Mastering Microsoft®

Teams®

Mastering Microsoft® Teams®

Creating a Hub for Successful Teamwork in Office 365

Christina Wheeler, Microsoft® MVP

Johnny Lopez, Microsoft® MVP

A Wiley Brand

This book is dedicated to my amazing daughter, Kiana. You are the most wonderful blessing to ever come into my life. I love you so much and am extremely proud of the amazing woman you have grown to become.
—Christina Wheeler

Acknowledgments

When I was first approached about writing a Teams book, I was hesitant. My biggest concern was that Teams is always changing. The entire Microsoft 365 suite and cloud products in general are ever-changing and evolving. Then it was pointed out that while features change, the concepts remain the same. I thought about it and decided to take it on. This is the first time I've written a book myself, which ended up being challenging due to the current times we are living in. I was thrown a lot of life curve balls and am grateful for Johnny Lopez stepping in to help get this book to the finish line. Speaking of finish line, my biggest thank you goes to my Development Editor, Adaobi Obi Tulton. Adaobi has been my partner through this entire project. She's been my rock, and there's no way I could have done this without her. I really appreciate the patience and hard work she's provided throughout the content and development of this project.

Thank you to my Technical Editor, Jon Buhagiar, for bringing his great perspective and for taking time out of his busy schedule to provide valuable technical feedback on all the chapters. I also want to thank Kenyon Brown, Acquisitions Editor, for reaching out on this proposal and for giving me the opportunity. I'm thankful for his patience and understanding as I went through life challenges that affected the timing of this project. I also want to thank the rest of the Sybex team for making this book possible: Christine O'Connor, Managing Editor; Saravanan Dakshinamurthy, Production Editor; Kim Cofer, Copyeditor; and the Compositors at Sybex.

About the Authors

Christina Wheeler (Microsoft® MVP) is currently a Director of Innovation at Core BTS. Prior to joining Core, she was a Principal Solution Architect for Canviz Consulting. Christina has always had a passion for technology, which started at a young age. At age 11, she used a Texas Instruments TI-99 plugged into a tape deck to copy BASIC code out of a book for hours so she and her brother could play games. At 13, her father taught her how to build computers. Christina initially went to a technical college for graphic design and video production. She worked in the print and marketing world for a while and then shifted to software and web development. She started out as a classic ASP developer in e-commerce then made her way into the auto and mortgage finance industry as a .NET developer. Christina got into the Business Intelligence space when she started filling in for a database administrator role. That's when she started working with Business Objects 6.5 and Crystal Reports. Then came SharePoint and that changed everything. Christina's first SharePoint project was a SharePoint 2001 portal and she's been working with SharePoint ever since.

Christina became a technical trainer when she started teaching for Mindsharp. She taught Todd Bleeker's custom SharePoint Development and SharePoint Web Content Management courses. During her time as an independent consultant, she specialized in Web Content Management (WCM) and built public-facing SharePoint publishing websites for customers. Christina was very good at making SharePoint not look like SharePoint. She also worked as a contracted trainer for Critical Path Training as an on-site and remote instructor for Ted Pattison's SharePoint, Power Apps, Power Automate, and Power BI courses. As a trainer, Christina brings her real-world experience to the classroom. Her publications include contributions as the technical editor of *SharePoint 2007 Developer's Guide to Business Data Catalog* (www.amazon.com/ SharePoint-Developers-Guide-Business-Catalog/dp/1933988819), co-author of the *SharePoint 2010 Field Guide* (www.amazon.com/SharePoint-2010-Field-Guide-Steven/ dp/1118105052), co-author of *SharePoint 2013 Inside Out* (www.amazon.com/ Microsoft-SharePoint-2013-Inside-Out/dp/0735666997), and co-author to *Office 365 for IT Pros*.

Before COVID-19, Christina traveled an average of 90,000 miles a year speaking at technology conferences around the world. Her last international speaking engagement was in March 2020 at TechDays Finland. She got into paddleboarding and VR fitness as her natural therapy during the pandemic, and her dogs are her constant companions.

Johnny Lopez (Microsoft® MVP) is a Microsoft Certified Trainer and a Principal Consultant at Core BTS on the Modern Workplace team. He is a passionate evangelist who delivers his professional experiences, technical expertise, and real-world Microsoft 365 content services and Power Platform experience to the technology communities. Johnny has been working in the SharePoint community for the last 10+ years. He served 10 years in the U.S. Navy serving on two aircraft carriers (USS *Eisenhower* and USS *Nimitz*) as an Electrical Work Center Supervisor. He graduated from the University of Phoenix of Houston in 2011 with a Bachelor of Science degree in Business Information Systems.

About the Technical Editor

Jon Buhagiar (Network+, A+, CCNA, MCSA, MCSE, BS/ITM) is an information technology professional with two decades of experience in higher education. During the past 22 years he has been responsible for Network Operations at Pittsburgh Technical College and led several projects, such as virtualization (server and desktop), VoIP, Microsoft 365, and many other projects supporting the quality of education at the college. He has achieved several certifications from Cisco, CompTIA, and Microsoft, and has taught many of the certification paths. He is the author of several books, including Sybex's *CompTIA Network+ Review Guide: Exam N10-008* 2021 and *CCNA Certification Practice Tests: Exam 200-301* 2020.

Contents at a Glance

Contents

Introduction

Microsoft Teams has become the hub for many organizations, and it has come a long way from when Microsoft launched the product on March 14, 2017. Teams primarily competes with a similar service, Slack, offering workspaces for chat, audio and video calls, file storage, and application integration with other services. While this book won't transform you into a Teams expert, it will help you understand basic features up to tenant-level admin features. This book begins by providing an overview of Teams and then goes into more details of the features broken down by chapter. First up is understanding how to create and manage teams, and then you'll learn about channels, chats, and apps functionality. Next, you will learn about the features and functionality for successful meetings and conferencing in Teams. Then you will learn options to extend Teams by integrating third-party and custom apps. You will also learn about the Teams admin center, which is geared toward those who want to understand what settings can be configured by the Teams tenant-level administrator. Even if you're not an administrator, it is helpful to understand what can be done. Lastly, the final chapter focuses on understanding settings at the admin tenant level for applying security, compliance, and governance policies.

The Mastering Series

The Mastering series from Wiley provides outstanding instruction for readers with intermediate and advanced skills, in the form of top-notch training and development for those already working in their field and clear, serious education for those aspiring to become pros. Every Mastering book features the following:

◆ The Wiley "by professionals for professionals" commitment. Mastering authors are themselves practitioners, with plenty of credentials in their areas of specialty.

◆ A practical perspective for a reader who already knows the basics—someone who needs solutions, not a primer.

◆ Skill-based instruction, with chapters organized around real tasks rather than abstract concepts or subjects.

◆ Self-review test "Master It" problems and questions, so you can be certain you're equipped to do the job right.

What Does This Book Cover?

Here is a glance at what's in each chapter. Jump to any chapter that you need to learn how to run Teams effectively.

Chapter 1: Getting to Know Microsoft Teams: This chapter provides a high-level overview of Microsoft Teams.

Chapter 2: Teams, Channels, Chats, and Apps: This chapter covers creating and managing teams, membership and roles, channels, chat features, and an overview of apps.

Chapter 3: Meetings and Conferencing: This chapter focuses on features and functionality for meetings and video conferencing in Teams. This includes managing and attending meetings, live events, webinars, breakout rooms, and audio conferencing.

Chapter 4: Extending Teams with Apps: This chapter dives deeper into apps in Teams, which includes Teams Apps capabilities, the types of apps that can be deployed, use case example of using a Teams app template, and ways to extend using the Power Platform.

Chapter 5: Administering Teams: This chapter covers the administration experience using the Microsoft Teams admin center. This includes settings for managing policies for meetings, users, teams, apps, and other Teams tenant-level admin settings.

Chapter 6: Security, Compliance, and Governance: This chapter provides a basic understanding of Teams security and features available for governing and applying policies for compliance.

Appendix A: Accessing Teams: The appendix covers installing the Teams app on the desktop and mobile devices, including modifying settings for your needs. It also covers accessing Teams through the browser and shows you how to install it as a browser app.

Who Should Read This Book

This book is intended for people newer to Microsoft Teams who want to learn about its core features, functionality, and capabilities. The goal of this book is to give you a solid foundation and understanding of the many things that Teams enables you to do to make working and collaborating with members of your team and others a more efficient and productive experience. While this book does cover admin-level settings and more advanced features, it is not intended to be a deep dive book. Much of the content is high-level with notes and resources for those who want to dive deeper into a specific topic.

Helpful Resources

Following are some helpful resources, including PDF guides for Microsoft Teams, online learning, and resources for Teams for Education:

◆ Matt Wade's Definitive Guide To: Rockstar Meetings in Microsoft Teams, `https://cdn.avepoint.com/pdfs/en/Rockstar-Meetings-in-Microsoft-Teams-eBook.pdf`

◆ Everyday Etiquette in Microsoft Teams in Government, `https://cdn.avepoint.com/pdfs/en/Etiquette-in-Teams-eBook-gov.pdf`

- Teams for Education, `https://docs.microsoft.com/en-us/microsoftteams/expand-teams-across-your-org/teams-for-education-landing-page`

- Microsoft Teams Help and Learning, `https://support.microsoft.com/en-us/teams?msclkid=ac092dedb69711ecb62658cb55239187`

- Microsoft Teams Online Video Training, `https://support.microsoft.com/en-us/office/microsoft-teams-video-training-4f108e54-240b-4351-8084-b1089f0d21d7?msclkid=da3d1146b69711eca17fc343657e8b7a`

- Microsoft Learn for Microsoft Teams, `https://docs.microsoft.com/en-us/learn/teams/?msclkid=fa930194b69711ecb790ffd7e8c5d06f`

How to Contact the Publisher

If you believe you have found a mistake in this book, please bring it to our attention. At John Wiley & Sons, we understand how important it is to provide our customers with accurate content, but even with our best efforts an error may occur.

In order to submit your possible errata, please email it to our Customer Service Team at `wileysupport@wiley.com` with the subject line "Possible Book Errata Submission."

Chapter 1

Getting to Know Microsoft Teams

Microsoft Teams has become a hot topic these days, especially with how our world changed in the year of 2020. We went from many people working on-site at their jobs to the entire world changing how they work due to COVID-19. When I first started writing this book, the world we live in looked entirely different. People were not working from home like they are today. Organizations have been forced to shift their way of thinking and change how their employees' work. With so many people now working remotely, many organizations are transitioning to Teams.

IN THIS CHAPTER, YOU WILL LEARN THE FOLLOWING

◆ Overview and benefits of Microsoft Teams

◆ Environmental readiness and driving user adoption

◆ Teams architecture

Overview of Microsoft Teams

Teams is a hub used for teamwork in Microsoft 365 where (if enabled) people inside and outside your organization can meet, chat, and collaborate in real time all in one place. Teamwork is an important aspect of the modern workplace and is a key element of enabling digital transformation within organizations. Whether from a mobile device, tablet (see Figure 1.1), or computer, you can easily run Teams no matter the platform.

FIGURE 1.1
Examples of Microsoft
Teams on devices

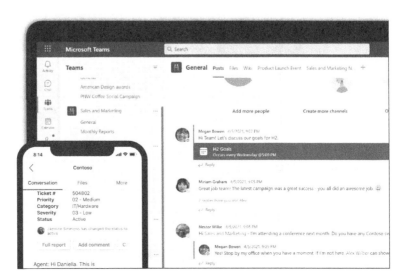

Key Benefits of Microsoft Teams

Teams has many feature benefits:

◆ **Hub for collaboration and teamwork in a modern workplace:** Organizations and teams across the globe are moving from working in offices to working remotely or adopting a hybrid workplace. Teams provides the ability to keep teams connected while users work apart by making Teams available globally.

◆ **Meeting experience:** Host online meetings as a 1:1 meeting, with a team (see Figure 1.2), or stream live events for up to 10,000 people with consistent experiences across platforms.

FIGURE 1.2
Teams meeting with group

You can take your meetings a step further with together mode. Together mode is a meeting feature that uses AI segmentation technology to digitally place participants in a shared background. This experience makes it feel like you are sitting in the same room with everyone else in the meeting or class (see Figure 1.3). Together mode helps make meetings more engaging by helping you focus on other people's facial expressions and body language. It's also great for meetings where multiple people will speak during brainstorming sessions and roundtables.

FIGURE 1.3
Teams meeting together mode

- **Instant messaging:** Connect instantly by using instant messaging one-on-one or with a group.

- **Calling:** With Teams calling you can implement Direct Routing and Calling Plans using Microsoft phone systems.

- **Devices:** Connect Teams through devices such as headsets, speakerphones, desk phones, room systems, conference phones, and certified Teams web cams.

- **Apps and workflows:** Teams is an extensible platform that allows you to integrate all types of apps within Teams. You can customize workspaces with tabs, connectors, and bots, as well as integrate your apps and automate workflows to fit your needs using Teams.

- **Distance learning:** Since in-person conferences have been shifted to online-only due to COVID-19, many have been using Teams to host their events. Smaller conferences have used the regular meetings feature while larger conferences have been using the Live Events feature for running sessions. For higher education, virtual classrooms can be created with Teams, which empower teachers to teach and students to learn virtually.

- **Frontline workers:** Many organizations that have frontline workers have been empowering their shift workers through using Teams.

- **Healthcare:** Healthcare workers can also be empowered to securely collaborate and communicate by helping clinicians and administrators perform their jobs more successfully with Teams.

- **Education:** Build collaborative classrooms, manage remote learning, enable a secure online classroom, on-demand webinars, and facilitate distance learning.

- **Security and compliance:** Teams comes with enterprise-grade security integrated with the Microsoft 365 Security and Compliance Center and Azure Active Directory. Teams safeguards your privacy by design by offering advanced security and compliance capabilities so you can collaborate without compromising security and privacy.

Teams for Work

Teamwork is an important aspect of a modern workplace and is a key element for enabling digital transformation within organizations. Teams brings together tools and communication methods that can fit the needs of a diverse workforce.

FRONTLINE WORKERS

Teams has been helping organizations digitally transform their frontline workers by creating a single hub for teamwork that provides a deeper connection across your organization (see Figure 1.4).

FIGURE 1.4
Microsoft Teams for
frontline workers

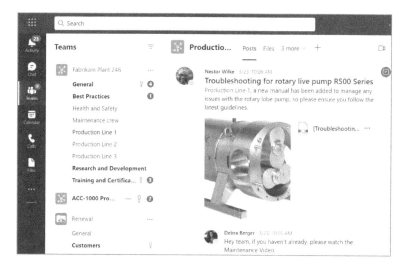

Walkie Talkie App in Microsoft Teams

Another way to equip frontline workers is with the Walkie Talkie app in Teams (see Figure 1.5).
This app allows your frontline workers to communicate securely with a familiar push-to-talk
(PTT) experience without the need to carry bulky radios. Walkie Talkie works anywhere with
Wi-Fi or cellular connectivity.

Shifts for Microsoft Teams

Shifts in Teams is a schedule management tool that provides the ability to create, update, and
manage schedules for team members backed by tools such as AMiON, BlueYonder, and Kronos.
Shifts features include:

◆ **Schedules:** Create a schedule from scratch or import an existing schedule from Excel. A
Shifts schedule displays days and team members (see Figure 1.6) and if you are an owner
of multiple teams, you can manage different Shifts schedules easily by toggling between
schedules.

◆ **Day Notes:** Add notes to share day reminders and important news.

◆ **Groups:** Name a group by a job function or location to keep groups organized then add
people to the groups.

◆ **Shifts:** Choose a slot to assign a shift. Create a shift from scratch or copy from an existing
one. Add activities such as training or a specific task. You can also add open shifts to a
schedule that anyone can request. If needing to review shift coverage, you can easily view
the schedule by people or shift type.

◆ **Requests:** Review requests for time-off, swap shifts, or offers.

◆ **Time Clock:** Turning this feature on enables team members to clock in and out of a shift
easily with a mobile device (see Figure 1.7). Enable location detection to ensure team
members clock in from a designated work site.

FIGURE 1.5
Teams Walkie Talkie

FIGURE 1.6
Teams Schedules

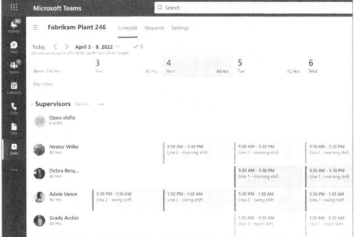

◆ **Share:** As you edit a schedule, the changes will be saved automatically but your team only sees the updates when you share it out.

◆ **Export or Copy:** You can export a schedule to Excel and if you need to reuse a Shifts schedule, you can copy it to the date range you want.

FIGURE 1.7
Teams Schedule Clock in

Tasks by Planner and To Do

Simplify the task management process with Tasks in Teams. The Tasks by Planner and To Do app in Teams is a feature that brings together your individual tasks from Planner and tasks from Microsoft To Do so you can more efficiently cross them off your list (see Figure 1.8).

FIGURE 1.8
Tasks by Planner
and To Do

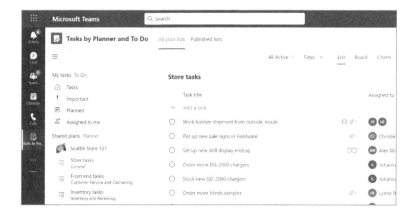

If your organization wants to streamline tasks for frontline workers, Tasks include capabilities that enable you to target, publish, and track tasks at a scale. Task publishing allows your organization to publish task lists targeted to specific locations (teams) across your entire organization to define and share a work plan to be completed at the locations. For example, anyone on the publishing team can create task lists and publish them to specific teams. Publishing can be done through the desktop or easily from a tablet or mobile device (see Figure 1.9). Managers of the recipients can review the published task lists and assign individual tasks to their team members (see Figure 1.10).

FIGURE 1.9
Publishing tasks
on a desktop

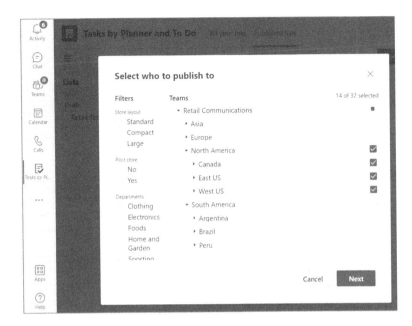

FIGURE 1.10
Assigning
team members

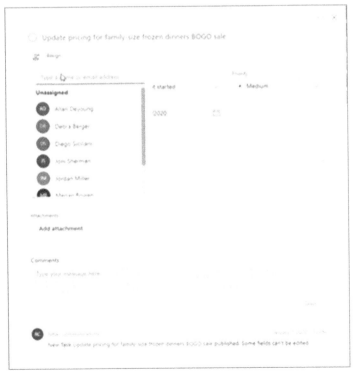

The Tasks by Planner and To Do app also has a feature that allows you to display tasks and information associated with them in rows and columns called a List view (see Figure 1.11).

FIGURE 1.11
List view

Task title	Assigned to		Priority	Due	Bucket ↓
		All Active ⌄ Filter ⌄ List Board Charts Schedule			
+ Add a task					
○ Negotiate pricing ... 🙂	EH Elva Hebert		↓	7/8	Pre-Process
○ Record supplier n... 🙂	EH Elva Hebert		!	7/11	Pre-Process
○ Evaluate supplie... ☐ 🙂	GG Greta Gilliam		↓	7/18	Pre-Process
○ Review suppliers s... 🙂	BB Brittney Beach		🔔	7/30	Pre-Process

NOTE Microsoft Teams provides a way for technology to unlock a new future for frontline workers. To read a study Microsoft published on how technology can provide a way to empower frontline workers, please visit `www.microsoft.com/en-us/worklab/work-trend-index/technology-unlocks-a-new-future-for-frontline`.

HEALTHCARE

Teams provides the ability to empower healthcare professionals with simple, secure collaboration and communication with chat, video, voice, and healthcare tools in a single hub that supports compliance with HIPAA, HITECH, and more. Bring together patients and clinicians with high-quality audio, video, and screensharing in a secure meeting experience to help support your telehealth workflows. Teams offers solutions for the entire healthcare organization:

◆ **Physicians:** Connect with patients (see Figure 1.12) and clinicians whether it is across your care team or health system through a multidisciplinary team (MDT) meeting or while on the go.

◆ **Nurses:** Orchestrate resources and care across departments, digitize clinical workflows, and enable coordinated care with instant access to people and patient information in a secure system.

◆ **Administrators:** Securely communicate with clinicians and all hospital staff across the organization and collaborate in one place.

FIGURE 1.12
Doctor with patient
Teams call

◆ **IT professionals:** Ensure clinicians and staff have a secure and compliant way to communicate and collaborate with built-in manageability features like eDiscovery, audit reports, and data loss prevention.

Connect instantly with secure messaging from the desktop, mobile device (see Figure 1.13), or tablet. Coordinate patient care in a single hub (see Figure 1.14).

FIGURE 1.13
Mobile secure messaging

FIGURE 1.14
Patient care hub

Embed Power BI reports easily in Teams (see Figure 1.15) with the trust that your data is secure. Built on the secure and compliant Microsoft 365 cloud, Teams enables HIPAA compliance and complies with standards like Health Information Trust Alliance (HITRUST), Service Organization Controls (SOC) 1 and 2, General Data Protection Regulation (GDPR), and more.

FIGURE 1.15
Power BI in Teams

Teams for Home

Microsoft Teams is not just for work—you can also use it with friends and family to stay connected across your life in the Teams mobile app. Friends and family can easily download the app (see Figure 1.16), which will enable them to use Teams for personal use. The app can be installed and used on a mobile device (see Figure 1.17) as well as a tablet.

FIGURE 1.16
Teams mobile app
download

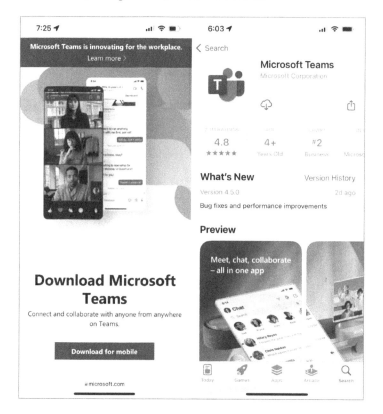

FIGURE 1.17
Teams mobile app

Already use Teams at work but you also have a personal account too? You can add your personal account to the desktop or mobile app so you can easily switch between your work and personal accounts to stay on top of calendars, chats, and tasks in and outside of work.

Teams for Education

Whether within the walls of the classroom or connecting remotely, educators can access the tools needed for classroom management and student engagement with Office 365 Education. Teams is empowering schools with the digital hub that brings conversations, content, assignments, and apps together in one place. Educators can build collaborative classrooms that allow them to quickly converse with students, share files, websites, distribute and grade assignments, as well as create a OneNote Class Notebook. Teams has clients available for desktop (Windows, Mac, and Linux), mobile (Android and iOS), and web-based so staff and students can stay connected no matter what platform educators and students are using.

Students and educators at eligible institutions can sign up for Office 365 Education for free. Included for free is Word, Excel, PowerPoint, OneNote, Microsoft Teams, and additional classroom tools. Students and educators can check if they are eligible by simply going online and entering their school email address. If not eligible, there are academic plan options available for purchase. Team types available to create include Class, Professional Learning Community (PLC), Staff, and Other (see Figure 1.18).

FIGURE 1.18
Creating teams for students and educators

CLASS TEAMS

Class teams (see Figure 1.19) provide special capabilities tailored for teaching and learning, which includes:

◆ Team with channels

◆ Class Notebook

◆ Assignments and Grades

◆ Ability to add tabs

◆ Share files

◆ Discussions, messaging options, and more

FIGURE 1.19
Teams tiles

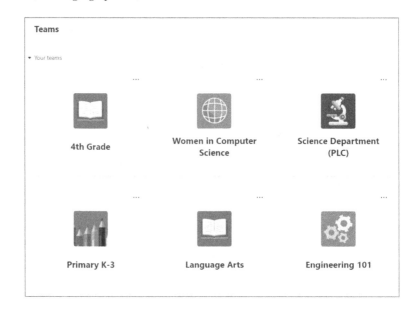

ASSIGNMENTS

Create learning activities and assignments (see Figure 1.20) for students with integrated Microsoft 365 applications. Add resources by customizing the assignment with content from OneDrive, your device, links, and more. Grading rubrics can add customizable, reusable rubrics for students to reference and for teachers to evaluate their work. Assignments can be distributed to multiple classes or personalized to the individual student (see Figure 1.21). Customize all dates and times that are important to the assignment.

FIGURE 1.20
Creating new assignment

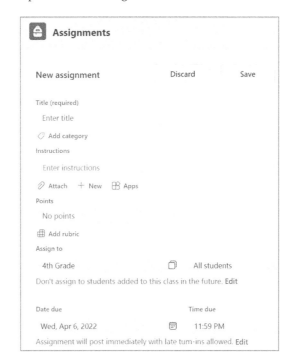

FIGURE 1.21
Assignments

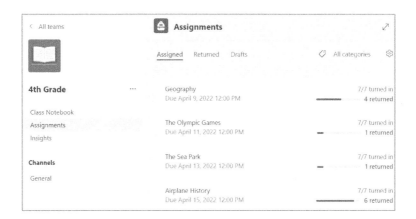

Files can be easily uploaded and will be available to the class members through the Files tab (see Figure 1.22).

FIGURE 1.22
Files tab with
assignments

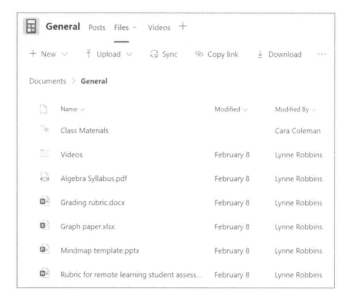

GRADES

Leave feedback for students, grade, and track progress. Each class team has a Grades tab, which provides a view to see all assignments at a glance, as well as track how individual students in the class are progressing (see Figure 1.23).

FIGURE 1.23
Reviewing student
assignments

Return and review assignments using the feedback loop (see Figure 1.24).

FIGURE 1.24
Return and review
assignments

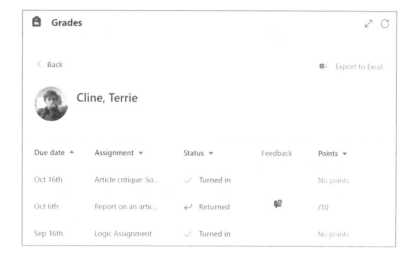

SOCIAL AND EMOTIONAL LEARNING

Educators can keep students engaged with Social and Emotional Learning (SEL) badges in the Praise app and with the SEL sticker pack for OneNote (see Figure 1.25). Encourage the development of critical life skills in the classroom while in a remote or hybrid learning environment.

FIGURE 1.25
SEL badges

STUDENTS

Students can easily access their online classroom right away in Office 365 Education and Teams using their school sign-in information. Once the student is logged in, they will see class team tiles under the list of Teams (see Figure 1.26).

FIGURE 1.26
Class team tiles

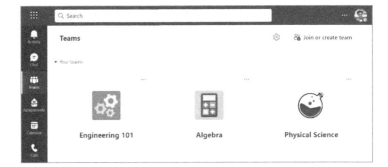

Every class team has a main discussion area under the General channel, and the Posts tab is where the teacher and classmates can start and reply to conversations (see Figure 1.27). The activity feed is a great way for students to ensure they do not miss a new assignment or an @ mention (see Figure 1.28).

FIGURE 1.27
Class group
conversations

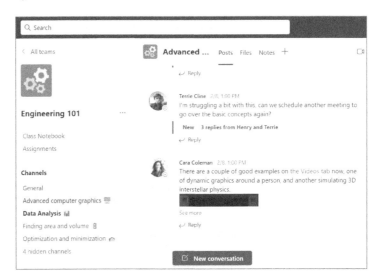

FIGURE 1.28
Activity feed
for students

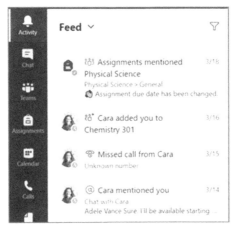

Microsoft Teams Collaboration and Acknowledgment

Whether you are using Teams for work, frontline workers, or education you can easily send praise to people to provide recognition for their efforts with the Praise app (see Figure 1.29). This app is one of the many great apps you can implement into Teams. We will cover more apps in detail in future chapters.

FIGURE 1.29
Praise app

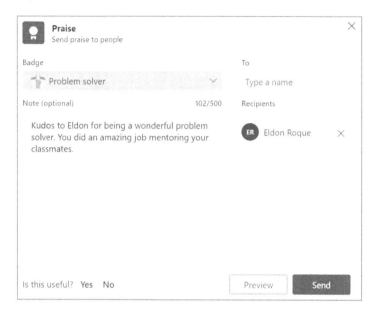

Another great feature in Teams is the ability to have a digital whiteboard. Microsoft Whiteboard is a free-form, digital canvas that allows Teams meeting participants to draw, sketch, and write together on a shared digital canvas (see Figure 1.30). While these are some of the features of Teams, we will dive further into more available features in later chapters.

FIGURE 1.30
Microsoft Whiteboard

Environmental Readiness and User Adoption

Now it is time to talk about environmental readiness and Teams user adoption. The best way to make adoption happen is through change management. Having a change management strategy for end-user awareness and adoption is critical to the successful rollout of Teams (and any new technology) within an organization.

Teams Adoption

One of the most important things when implementing Teams is driving user adoption. By driving adoption of Teams, you can deliver an exceptional user experience and increase business value inside your organization.

There are three main phases for driving Teams user adoption (see Figure 1.31):

FIGURE 1.31
User adoption phases

◆ **Start:** This is the first phase where you gather your team together, set up your initial teams, and start using Teams to begin planning Teams adoption. This will help you and your adoption team increase your technical familiarity with the product and help you build the necessary skills to successfully complete each phase.

◆ **Experiment:** This is the phase where you bring early adopters and internal champions on board. Speak to the business users to identify scenarios that would immediately benefit from the communication and collaboration capabilities of Teams. The feedback gathered will help inform your broad-scale adoption phase and to make service decisions about governance and life-cycle management that will ensure a successful deployment.

◆ **Scale:** This is the phase where you will turn on Teams capabilities for all users in a broad-scale deployment phase. During this phase, the size of your organization will determine the approach you will take for the deployment. Depending on the size of your organization you will either "go big" turning on Teams for all users simultaneously, or approach it by regions, business units, or other methods segmenting your rollout based on employee population.

In this phase you will also move to a continuous delivery model. As employees, business units, and leaders will want to expand their use of Teams, they will require training and your engagement to understand best how to use Teams and other features of Microsoft 365.

PHASE 1: START

The primary goal of the start phase is to ensure readiness for the experimentation phase. During this phase you will determine if assistance from Microsoft or from a network of skilled partners is needed. Microsoft does provide a guided deployment feature called Teams advisor. This feature can be accessed by the Teams administrator in the Microsoft Teams admin center under Planning. The Teams advisor is a planning feature that creates a workspace for the Microsoft Teams deployment team.

Champions are an essential part to drive awareness, adoption, and to help educate users within your organization. A champion is a person motivated to help others and interested in new technologies such as Teams. Champions fit into your overall launch planning for Teams. Champions should:

◆ Be trained formally to increase their depth of knowledge in the product.

◆ Be empowered and encouraged to guide, teach, and train others.

◆ Have consistent and positive reinforcement as well as a clear plan to execute.

PHASE 2: EXPERIMENT

The experiment phase can vary across organizations and the recommendation is to implement what works best for you and your team. Whether your organization is large or small, the recommendation is to complete this phase to help gain insight into how Teams can improve collaboration within your organization beyond chat and file storage features. By using Teams for experimenting with a few real-world projects within your group that is led by a stakeholder, you will be able to get meaningful feedback that will help you make decisions for org-wide implementation.

PHASE 3: SCALE

In the scale phase you use what you have learned in the previous stages to support a broad-scale enablement of Teams within your organization. Microsoft has identified the steps of the phase as the following:

◆ Define outcomes and success measures.

◆ Select service strategy.

◆ Engage stakeholders.

◆ Design and launch an awareness campaign.

◆ Design and launch a training program.

◆ Understand reporting tools.

◆ Prepare for ongoing business engagement.

◆ Prepare for ongoing service health & adoption reviews.

There are four categories of outcome that can be prioritized for your organization, which are interconnected and form the foundation of the modernization and digital transformation each individual Teams user will experience (see Figure 1.32).

FIGURE 1.32
Outcome categories

Some examples of outcomes for each of the categories include:

◆   Organizational:

  ◆   Cultural transformation & employee retention

  ◆   Talent acquisition

  ◆   Social engagement

  ◆   Operational agility

◆   Cultural:

  ◆   Employee sentiment & recommendations

  ◆   Customer feedback

  ◆   Innovation measures (for example, roundtables, hackathons, product innovation engagements)

◆   Tangible:

  ◆   Customer experience impacts (customer referral/loyalty program participation)

  ◆   Cost savings & revenue generation

  ◆   Data security, process simplification, and retirement of legacy systems

◆ Individual:

   ◆ Use of desired tools

   ◆ Employee morale, productivity, and engagement

   ◆ Idea generation

NOTE   For more information and helpful tools for user adoption, please visit `https://adoption` `.microsoft.com/microsoft-teams`.

For industry and role scenario Microsoft playbooks, please visit `https://adoption.microsoft` `.com/microsoft-teams/industry-and-role-scenario-playbooks`.

Teams Architecture

Teams is built on Microsoft 365 groups and Microsoft Graph. It uses the same enterprise-level security compliance and manageability as Microsoft 365. Identities are stored in Azure Active Directory (Azure AD) and Teams works both online and offline. When you create a new team in Teams, the following are created:

◆ A Microsoft 365 group, which handles the membership of the team.

◆ A SharePoint Online site and document library used to store team files.

◆ An Exchange Online shared mailbox and calendar.

◆ A OneNote notebook that is stored in the SharePoint Online site and surfaced inside Teams.

When you create a team from an existing Microsoft 365 group, you get the following:

◆ The existing Microsoft 365 group's membership.

◆ A SharePoint Online site and document library used to store team files.

◆ The existing Exchange Online shared mailbox and calendar.

◆ A OneNote notebook that is stored in the SharePoint Online site and surfaced inside Teams.

Teams and Microsoft 365

The logical architecture consists of the Teams client, OneDrive for Business, SharePoint Online, Microsoft Planner, Exchange Online, Microsoft Stream, and optionally Yammer (see Figure 1.33).

FIGURE 1.33
Teams logical
architecture

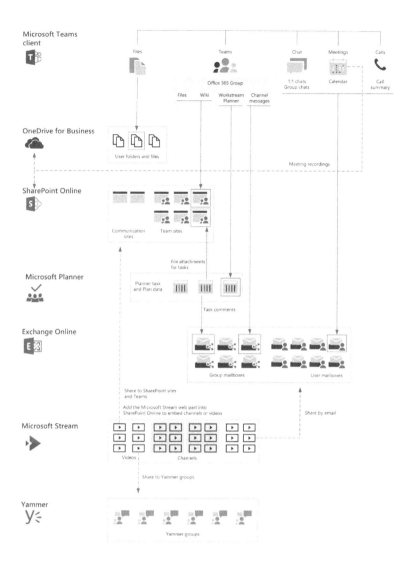

NOTE For more detailed diagrams on the logical architecture, please visit https://aka.ms/
TeamsArchSolutionsPosters and https://aka.ms/CloudArchModels.

The Bottom Line

Benefits of Teams The modern workplace has changed drastically since 2020. Most employees, customers, vendors, and contractors are working remotely from their home where they miss the in-person collaboration or what we like to call "cooler talk." Teams provides the flexibility of instant collaboration and empowers users to connect with colleagues and even people they need to communicate with outside of their organization.

Master It   Your organization has a vast majority of employees working from home or in other remote locations. There is a need to work with internal colleagues and outside vendors to complete their daily assigned tasks.

Environmental readiness and driving user adoption   The key to a successful deployment of Teams is making sure the organization is in the highest readiness situation as possible. This includes ensuring that the planning, communication, and training being provided is seamless and transparent to the organization leadership, champions, help desk, and information workers.

Master It   The marketing department has a requirement to collaborate with a third-party video editing firm. They need to share marketing videos to be edited in a safe and secure manner.

Teams architecture   The Teams platform was made for enhancing communication and collaboration in the modern workplace. Microsoft is constantly improving the platform to better enable organizations to streamline business processes, meet virtually combined with in-person meetings, and deliver an industry-leading solution for external sharing.

Master It   The production group has a need to train their employees to meet a regular compliance policy required by the federal government. They need to set up training sessions, provide employees with a registration form, and store the training recording in one place.

Chapter 2

Teams, Channels, Chats, and Apps

One of the challenges organizations had before Teams was drowning in emails with email-upon-email responses. People were challenged with the back and forth in emails to coordinate when to meet and what platform to use. Drowning in emails is becoming a thing of the past. As more organizations are using Teams, it's making it so much easier for people to have structured conversations as well as meet inside and outside their organization. Microsoft Teams consists of teams, channels, chats, and apps. You can use the basic features to communicate and collaborate, or you can extend the functionality by integrating apps in Teams to automate workflows and other business processes based on your needs.

IN THIS CHAPTER, YOU WILL LEARN THE FOLLOWING

- ◆ Overview of teams, channels, chats, and apps
- ◆ Team membership and roles
- ◆ Managing teams
- ◆ Working with channels
- ◆ Microsoft Teams templates
- ◆ User presence in Microsoft Teams

Overview of Teams, Channels, Chats, and Apps

Teams is an evolving product that will continue to grow as Microsoft enhances and adds new functionality. The purpose of this chapter is to help you understand the core functionality of teams, channels, chats, and apps.

Teams and Channels

In Microsoft Teams, a team is a collection of people brought together for work, projects, or common interests. A team can be dynamic for project-based work or ongoing for your organizational needs. Teams are built on Microsoft 365 groups and can be created in two ways:

- ◆ Created to be private to only invited users.
- ◆ Created to be public and open so anyone within the organization can join.

Currently, you can have up to 10,000 members in an org-wide team. Microsoft Yammer can be used for organizations that need org-wide collaboration with over 10,000 users. Microsoft Yammer has a limitation of 500,000 users versus 10,000 in Microsoft Teams. Teams consist of channels (see Figure 2.1). Channels are dedicated sections within a team to keep conversations organized. Each channel is built around a topic and are where you have conversations, hold meetings, and collaborate on files.

FIGURE 2.1
Teams and channels

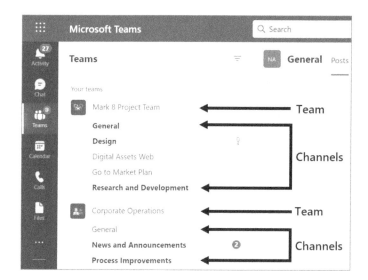

Channels can be open to all members of a team or targeted for a select audience. Conversations, notes, and files across channels are only visible to team owners and members. The access also is dependent on the type of channel you create. You can create three types of channels in a team (see Figure 2.2):

Standard: Standard channels are for conversations that everyone in a team can participate in. They are open and accessible to everyone on the team. By default, all members of a team can create standard channels.

Private: Private channels are intended for conversations that are only accessible to a specific group of people that have been granted access.

Shared: Shared Channels are for conversations with people inside and outside of the team. Only shared channel owners and members of the shared channel can access the channel.

PRIVATE CHANNELS

By default, private channels can be created by a team owner or team member. The Teams administrator can, however, change the permissions and limit the creation of private channels by role in your tenant. Behind the scenes, each private channel has its own SharePoint site and is linked to the parent team.

FIGURE 2.2
Create channel
drop-down menu for
choosing channel type.

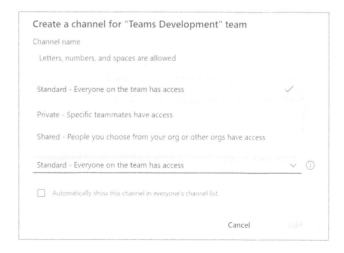

When a private channel is added to a team it will have a lock icon to indicate the channel is private (see Figure 2.3). The person who creates the private channel becomes the private channel owner. All members of the team do not automatically gain access to the private channel; the access must be granted by the owner of the private channel or by a member of the channel (if enabled). You can grant people access to a private channel only if they are already a member of the team. If they are not a member of the team and you want to grant them access to the private channel, you must add them as a member to the team first.

FIGURE 2.3
Private channel
showing lock icon

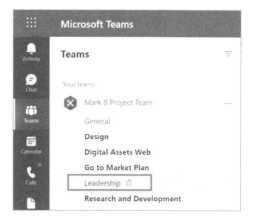

Team members can only see private channels of which they are a member. Team owners can see the names of all private channels that exist in the team they own. If the owner is not a member of a private channel, they will not be able to see the files, conversations, or members of the channel, but they can delete it. Deleted channels can be restored within 30 days of being deleted.

You can have more than one owner to a private channel, and a private channel owner cannot be removed through the Teams client if they are the last owner of the channel. On the other hand, if a private channel owner leaves your organization and is removed from the Microsoft 365 group associated with the team, a member of the private channel will automatically be promoted to be the private channel owner. If a team member is still within the organization but is only removed from a team with private channels, the user will automatically be removed from the private channels of which they were members. If the user is added back to the team, they will have to be added back manually to the private channels they were members of before.

NOTE To read about the current private channel limitations, please visit `https://docs.microsoft.com/en-us/MicrosoftTeams/private-channels#private-channel-limitations`.

SHARED CHANNELS

Shared channels have been one of the most requested features for Teams. At the time of writing this, shared channels have become available through public preview. This means you may not see this feature in your organizational tenant unless your Teams admin has enabled public preview. When the feature is enabled in your tenant, you will be able to create a shared channel by selecting it from the Private drop-down list (see Figure 2.4). Once created, you will see a chain link icon next to the channel name (see Figure 2.5).

FIGURE 2.4
Creating a shared channel dialog example

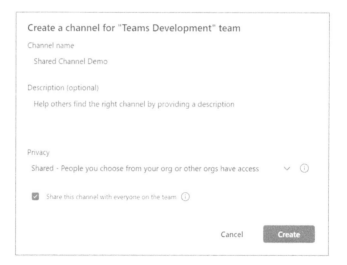

FIGURE 2.5
Shared channel example in a team

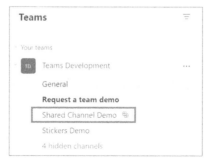

NOTE   Shared channels are currently in preview. To read more about shared channels, please visit `https://docs.microsoft.com/en-us/MicrosoftTeams/shared-channels`.

Fellow Microsoft MVP, Tony Redmond published a great article on the new Teams Shared Channels. To read his article "Diving into the Details of Microsoft Teams Shared Channels", please visit `https://practical365.com/microsoft-prepares-debut-teams-shared-channels/`.

Azure Active Directory (AD) B2B direct connect is required if you want to invite people outside of your organization to participate in a shared channel. To read more about Azure AD B2B direct connect, please visit `https://docs.microsoft.com/en-us/azure/active-directory/external-identities/b2b-direct-connect-overview`.

DEFAULT TEAM, CHANNELS, AND FEATURES

When a team is created from scratch, it will contain a default channel called General and three tabs, which include Posts, Files, and Wiki. The Posts tab is a default tab for general channel conversations. These conversations are accessible to all members of the team (see Figure 2.6).

FIGURE 2.6
Conversations in Teams in a General channel

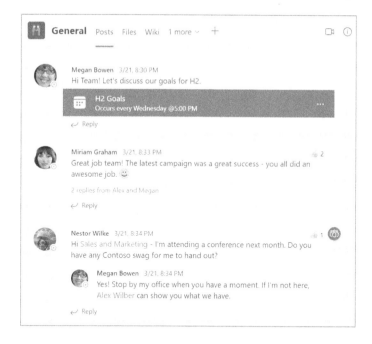

Files Tab

As mentioned in Teams Architecture section in the first chapter, when a team is created in Teams it includes a SharePoint Online site with a document library that is used to store the team files. This document library is located in the Files tab at the top of each channel (see Figure 2.7). You can create new folders as well as files by clicking New (see Figure 2.8).

FIGURE 2.7
Files tab surfacing
SharePoint docu-
ment library

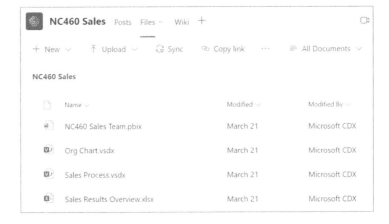

FIGURE 2.8
Creating new files in
Teams channel
drop-down

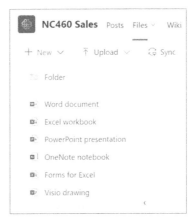

You can work with the files directly in Teams through the Files tab or work with them in the team's SharePoint site by clicking Open in SharePoint (see Figure 2.9 and Figure 2.10). There are times you may need to use the team's SharePoint site to manage files if a feature is not available in Teams. For instance, Teams supports copying and moving files around in a team but if you need to copy or move folders, that feature is only available in SharePoint Online.

FIGURE 2.9
Open In SharePoint

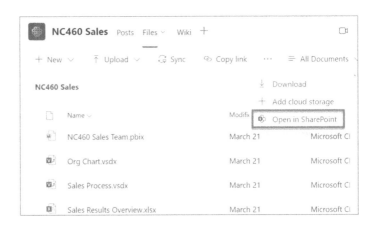

FIGURE 2.10
Teams files opened in
the SharePoint site

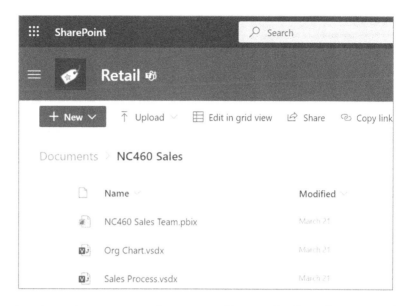

Files that you share in a private or group chat are stored in your OneDrive for Business folder
and are only shared with people in the conversation. These are found in the Files tab at the top of
a chat. To share files to the private or group chat, you would need to click Share and then select
OneDrive or Upload From My Computer (see Figure 2.11).

FIGURE 2.11
OneDrive for
Business dialog

Wiki Tab

The Wiki tab is generated by default. Wiki is a smart-text editor that doubles as a communication
machine where you draft, edit, and chat all in one place. This tab is not required to be used and
you can decide to remove it or use it for things such as frequently asked questions (FAQs) or
instructional information. The initial content of the Wiki tab will contain placeholder text for you
to replace for naming the page, creating sections, and adding content to the sections (see
Figure 2.12). You can easily add sections and content by clicking on New Page or Add a New
Section Here (see Figure 2.13), as well as move up/down and delete sections (see Figure 2.14).

FIGURE 2.12
Wiki page placeholder
text and sections

FIGURE 2.13
Add New Page and Add a
New Section Here links

FIGURE 2.14
Moving Wiki
page sections

NOTE For more information on how to work with the Wiki tab,
please visit https://support.microsoft.com/en-us/office/add-and-use-a-wiki-tabin-
teams-35ec762d-72ec-4d7f-b858-2949f6cb6014.

To read about 8 tips for creating a wiki everyone will use, please visit
www.microsoft.com/en-us/microsoft-365/business-insights-ideas/resources/
8-tips-for-creating-a-wiki-everyone-will-use.

LIMITATIONS OF TEAMS AND CHANNELS

Teams and channels do have some limitations. While these could change in the future, the
current limitations are:

◆ Number of teams a user can create is subject to a 250 limit.

◆ Maximum number of teams a global administrator can create is 500,000.

◆ Maximum number of teams an M365 or O365 organization can have is 500,000.

◆ Maximum number of teams a user can be a member of is 1,000.

- Maximum number of members allowed in a standard or private team is 25,000.

- Maximum number of members in org-wide team is 10,000.

- Number of org-wide teams allowed in tenant is 5.

- Maximum number of owners allowed per team is 100.

- Number of channels per team:

  - Standard channels maximum is 200 per team. This number includes deleted channels.

  - Private channels maximum is 30 channels per team. This number includes deleted channels.

- Maximum number of members in an O365 group that can be converted to a team is 10,000.

- Channel conversation post size limit is approximately 28K per post.

- For GCC tenants, the maximum number of members in a team is 25,000. GCCH/DoD tenants can only accommodate 2,500 members per team.

Current limitations for Channel names:

- Channel names cannot contain the following characters: ~ # % & * { } + / \ : < > ? | ' ", ..

- Characters not allowed in this range: 0 to 1F and 80 to 9F

- Words not allowed: forms, CON, CONIN$, CONOUT$, PRN, AUX, NUL, COM1 to COM9, LPT1 to LPT9, desktop.ini, _vti_

NOTE To read more on teams and channels limitations, please visit https://docs.microsoft .com/en-us/microsoftteams/limits-specifications-teams#teams-and-channels.

Chats

In addition to having conversations in channels, Teams also enables conversations outside of channels called chats. Chats in Teams can be one-on-one or in a group. To start a one-on-one or group chat, you simply click the New Chat icon and then input the individual or group of individuals you'd like to start the chat with (see Figure 2.15). The benefit of using chat in Teams is being able to cut down on email communication for conversations that should be more chat-driven.

FIGURE 2.15
Starting a chat in Teams

ONE-ON-ONE CHAT

Once you've entered the person's name for a one-on-one chat you can compose your message in the box at the bottom of the chat (see Figure 2.16). To open your formatting options, select the Format button beneath the box where you type your message to expand the formatting toolbar (see Figure 2.17). You can select this toggle to expand/collapse the formatting toolbar at any time.

FIGURE 2.16
Starting a new conversation

FIGURE 2.17
Compose message

GROUP CHAT

You can use group chat when you need to have a conversation with a small group of people. You can start a group chat by adding multiple people or a Microsoft 365 group into the To field or click the down arrow for more options (see Figure 2.18).

FIGURE 2.18
Drop-down arrow for more chat options

The additional options for the group chat will provide a field to set the group name and a To field to add people to the chat (see Figure 2.19 and Figure 2.20).

FIGURE 2.19
Group name

FIGURE 2.20
Adding people to
group chat

When the group chat is created, you will notice it looks different than a one-on-one chat (see Figure 2.21).

FIGURE 2.21
Group chat

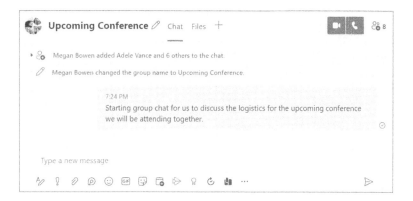

Group chats will have an icon showing how many people have been added to the conversation, as well as a Chat and a Files tab. When you click the members icon you will see all the people included in the conversation and have an option to add people or leave the conversation (see Figure 2.22).

You can add people to an existing group chat. If a conversation has already started, you will be prompted with chat history options. The default is set to Don't Include Chat History, so be sure you change this option if you want to include the chat history for the people you are adding to the conversation (see Figure 2.23).

If the group chat has been created but no conversations have started, you will only be prompted to add additional people without chat history options (see Figure 2.24).

FIGURE 2.22
Managing people in
group chat

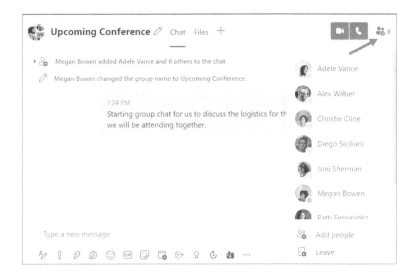

FIGURE 2.23
Adding people to group
chat with chat his-
tory options

FIGURE 2.24
Adding people without
chat history options

LIMITATIONS OF CHATS

There are some limitations for using chat in Teams. One of the requirements for users to be able to participate in chat is that they must have an Exchange Online (cloud-based) mailbox. This is required because conversations for one-on-one and group chats are stored in the cloud-based mailboxes of chat participants:

- Maximum number of people allowed in a private chat is 250.

- Maximum number of people allowed in a video or audio call triggered from a chat is 20.

- Maximum number of file attachments allowed in a chat is 10.

- Maximum number of chat size is approximately 28k per post.

NOTE To read more on teams and channels limitations, please visit `https://docs.microsoft`
`.com/en-us/microsoftteams/limits-specifications-teams#chat`.

Teams Apps

Now that you have a basic understanding of teams, channels, and chats, let's talk about Teams apps. Channels are most valuable when extended with apps that include tabs, connectors, and bots, which increases the value to the members of the team. Many different types of apps can be deployed in Teams. This includes Microsoft apps, third-party apps, and custom developed apps (see Figure 2.25).

FIGURE 2.25
Types of apps for Teams

MICROSOFT APPS

A variety of Microsoft apps are available and many are already deeply integrated into Teams (see Figure 2.26).

FIGURE 2.26
Microsoft
apps for Teams

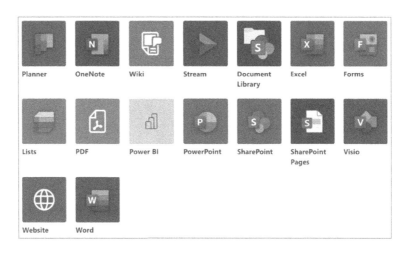

THIRD-PARTY APPS

You can choose from over 1,000 popular apps available in the Teams app store to make your work easier every day (see Figure 2.27).

FIGURE 2.27
Teams app store

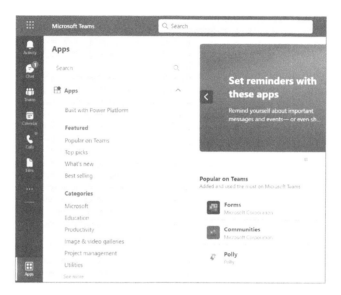

Some of the types of apps available for Teams include:

Productivity apps: Increase your team's productivity with workflow and process automation apps to simplify how work gets done.

Project management apps: Easily navigate complex projects using process automation apps and tools.

Industry-specific apps: Address industry-specific needs with custom-built apps.

Business department apps: Execute everyday responsibilities with job-specific apps.

CUSTOM APPS

The core workloads in Teams include the ability to communicate through chats, meetings, and calls as well as collaborate with deeply integrated Office 365 apps. While other tools are available in the market that you can use to communicate and collaborate, the big question is what sets Teams apart from others. The answer to that is through the Teams extensible platform. The extensible platform enables you to do more by connecting all your systems and processes through third-party apps and custom apps (see Figure 2.28).

FIGURE 2.28
Core workloads

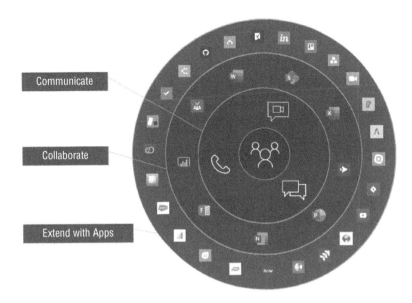

Communicate

Collaborate

Extend with Apps

Low-Code Solutions

You can quickly build custom apps and digital tools for Teams, with little or no development experience. Low-code solution apps include:

◆ **Power Apps:** Create custom apps to digitize processes and improve efficiency (see Figure 2.29).

◆ **Power Automate:** Automate repetitive tasks and connect data to improve agility and productivity.

◆ **Power Virtual Agents:** Build low-code chatbots to provide conversational, AI-driven insights and information.

◆ **Power BI:** Discuss and visualize data to align teams and confidently make data-driven decisions.

Professional Developer Apps

You can develop custom app solutions for Microsoft Teams to meet your business needs. Custom app solutions include:

◆ **Developer tools:** Enjoy frictionless app development with using Microsoft Teams toolkits.

◆ **Extensibility points:** Expand the reach of your app with tabs, bots, and messaging extensions.

◆ **User Interface (UI) Elements:** Create rich experiences with adaptive cards, task modules, and notifications.

◆ **Application programming interfaces (APIs):** Use Microsoft Graph to enhance apps inside and outside of Teams.

FIGURE 2.29
Power Apps in Teams
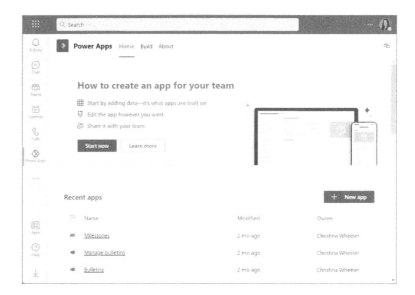

This is a high-level overview of custom apps. More in-depth coverage of the Teams develop-ment platform and the how-to for custom apps will be covered in Chapter 4, "Extending Teams with Apps."

Best Practices

Now that we have covered an overview of teams, channels, chats, and apps, let's talk about some best practice recommendations for organizing files in channels and working with group chats.

FILES TAB

Whether you are working with the General channel or a new custom channel, it is recommended you define your folder structure in the Files tab. When team members want to upload files to the channel, encourage them to store them in the proper folder and send a link from that file once it's stored. Using folders to help organize the files makes it cleaner and prevents you from having a bunch of files hanging out in the root. If you don't set up a structure initially and decide to sort them out later, links to files in current conversations will become broken.

GROUP CHATS

While it's not required to name your group chats, the best practice recommendation is to set a group name. Naming your group chats makes it easier to keep track of them. This also helps make it clear what the subject of the conversation is. Once you name a chat on creation, you can change the name any time after a conversation has been started within the chat (see Figure 2.30).

There may be times you want to keep track of a conversation for quick access within Teams. You can do this by pinning a one-on-one or group chat. You can pin up to 15 chats and drag each pinned chat in the order you want. It's common practice to pin chats temporarily and then unpin the chat when you don't need it front and center anymore (see Figure 2.31).

FIGURE 2.30
Changing
group chat name

FIGURE 2.31
Pinning and
unpinning chats

Team Membership and Roles

As mentioned earlier in this chapter, Teams is based on Microsoft 365 groups. Microsoft 365 groups work with Azure Active Directory and are the foundational membership service that drives teamwork across Microsoft 365. Groups allow you to set up a collection of people (known as members) to provide access to shared resources. These shared resources include:

- Shared Outlook inbox
- Shared calendar
- SharePoint document library

◆   Planner

◆   OneNote notebook

◆   Power BI

◆   Yammer (if groups were created from Yammer)

◆   Team (if group was created from Teams)

The benefit of Microsoft 365 groups is that you do not have to manually assign permissions for each person. The permissions are handled at the group level. When you add people to the group, the group automatically assigns the permissions needed to the people who have been added to the group.

While you can create Microsoft 365 groups in many ways, this chapter focuses on creating groups for Teams. When you create a team from scratch in Teams, it will create a new Microsoft 365 group. As you add users to the team, it will add the users to the Microsoft 365 group for access. If you create a team from an existing Microsoft 365 group, any changes made to the group will be synced with Microsoft Teams automatically. Creating a team based on an existing Microsoft 365 group simplifies the process of inviting and managing members and syncs group files inside of Microsoft Teams.

Every member in Teams has a role, and each role has different permissions. The roles available in Microsoft Teams are:

Team owner   Person who creates the team. Team owners can manage certain settings for a team. They can add/remove team members and guests (if enabled) and change team settings. Owners can also handle administrative tasks.

Team owners can also make any member of their team a co-owner. Having multiple team owners allows you to share the responsibilities of managing settings, membership, and invitations.

Team members   People who the owners invite to join their team. Members are the people in the team and have limited permissions. Team members can talk with other team members in conversations and collaborate in the channels they have access to.

Guests   People from outside of your organization that a team owner invites; these are typically partners, vendors, consultants, or customers. Guests have fewer capabilities than team members or team owners, and guests are only allowed if guest access has been enabled at the tenant level. You can find more details on guest access in Chapter 5, "Administering Teams."

Creating and Managing Teams

As an admin, you can create and manage teams within the Teams admin center or directly in the Teams client. You can create a team from scratch (see Figure 2.32), from a group or team, or from a template (see Figure 2.33). Templates are discussed further in "Teams Templates" later in this chapter and the Teams admin center is covered in Chapter 5. When you create a team from scratch or from a template you will be prompted to choose the privacy level of the team. The choices include Private or Public (see Figure 2.34).

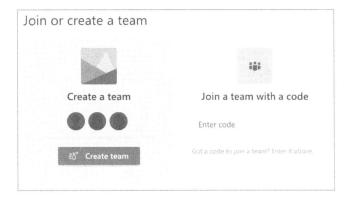

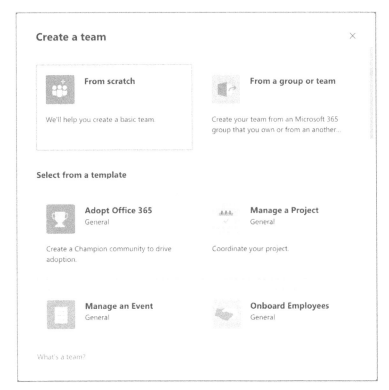

Org-wide Teams

Org-wide teams provide a way for everyone within the organization to automatically be a part of a public team for collaboration. When an org-wide team is created, the team pulls in all users within the organization and keeps the membership up-to-date with Azure Active Directory. When users join or leave the organization, the membership in Teams is automatically updated. Only global Teams tenant admins can create org-wide teams, and org-wide teams are currently limited to organizations with no more than 10,000 users. There's also a limit of 5 org-wide teams per tenant. When these requirements are met, global admins will see Org-wide as an option when they select Build A Team From Scratch when creating a team (see Figure 2.35).

FIGURE 2.34
Private or Public create team option

FIGURE 2.35
Org-wide option

When an org-wide team is created, all global admins and Teams service administrators are added as team owners. All active users are added as team members, and unlicensed users are also added to the org-wide team. Unlicensed users will be assigned a Microsoft Teams Exploratory license when they first sign in. These types of accounts won't be added to your org-wide team:

♦ Accounts that are blocked from signing in

♦ Guest users

♦ Resource or service accounts

♦ Room or equipment accounts

♦ Accounts backed by a shared mailbox

NOTE   To learn more about the Microsoft Teams Exploratory license, please visit `https://docs` `.microsoft.com/en-us/microsoftteams/teams-exploratory`.

Team Settings

Team owners can manage team-wide settings directly within Microsoft Teams. Options available in the menu are dependent on the user's role. When a team owner clicks the menu for a team, they will be provided with additional links that a team member would not have. This includes Manage Team, Edit Team, and Delete The Team (see Figure 2.36).

FIGURE 2.36
Manage team options
drop-down menu choices

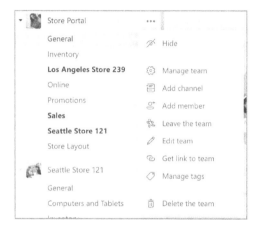

EDIT TEAM

The Edit Team option allows team owners to change the Team Name, Description, and Privacy setting of the team (see Figure 2.37).

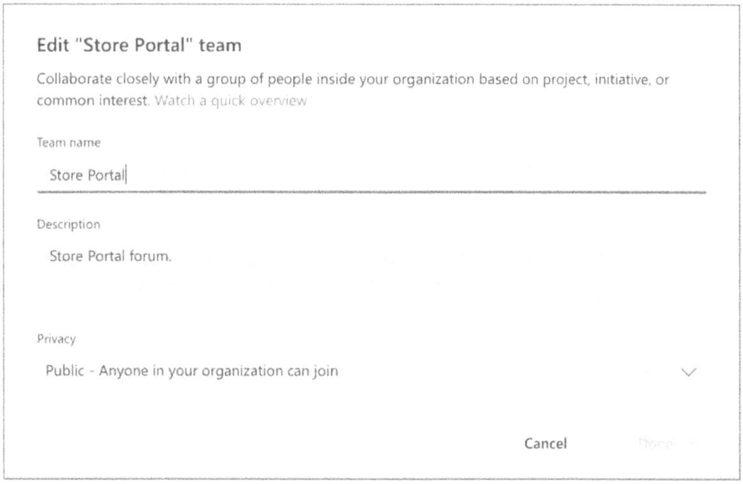

FIGURE 2.37
Editing team name,
description, and
privacy settings

Edit "Store Portal" team

Collaborate closely with a group of people inside your organization based on project, initiative, or common interest. Watch a quick overview

Team name

Store Portal

Description

Store Portal forum.

Privacy

Public - Anyone in your organization can join   ⌄

Cancel   Done

Members

The Members tab is used for managing the team membership. This includes the ability to add, remove, and change membership roles for owners, team members, and guests (see Figure 2.38).

FIGURE 2.38
Viewing members of
team settings where you
can add and
delete members

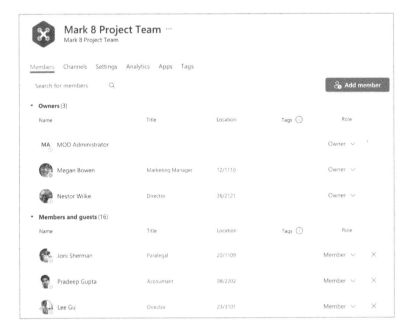

Channels

The Channels tab for a team is where team owners can hide, show, add, and delete channels (see Figure 2.39). The Show For Me setting is a personal view setting that only affects you seeing channels within your team. Each user has this setting; they can use it to hide/show channels by default. The Show For Members setting allows you to automatically show channels for all members of the team.

FIGURE 2.39
Channels tab settings

	Mark 8 Project Team ···					
	Mark 8 Project Team					

Members Channels Settings Analytics Apps Tags

Search for channels   🔍   🔲 **Add channel**

▾ **Active** (5)

Name ▲	Show for me	Show for members	Description	Type	Last activity	
General				🌐	4/18/2021	···
Design	☑	☐	Discuss design projects	🌐	4/18/2021	···
Digital Ass…	☑	☑	Discuss digital assets	🌐	4/18/2021	···
Go to Mar…	☑	☐	Our go-to-market plan!	🌐	4/18/2021	···
Research a…	☑	☐	Channel for Research and Develop…	🌐	4/18/2021	···

SETTINGS

The Settings tab is where team owners can change the team picture, member permissions, guest permissions, @mentions, team code, fun stuff, and tag settings (see Figure 2.40).

FIGURE 2.40
Settings tab settings

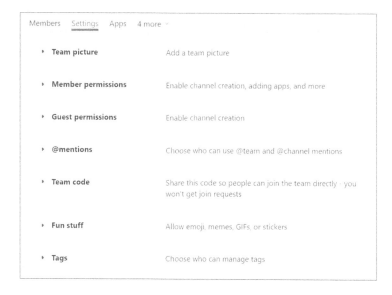

Team Picture

When a team is created, it is not automatically created with a picture. A picture can be added or changed anytime under the Team Picture section (see Figure 2.41). A common practice is to set the image based on the type of team. For example, if you are using Teams to manage client projects and have a team for each client then you may want to set the team picture to the client's logo.

FIGURE 2.41
Changing team picture

Member Permissions

The Member Permissions section includes various toggle settings for what you want to allow members to do within the team (see Figure 2.42). By default, all permissions are enabled for the team members. However, you can turn off any of the settings by unchecking the box next to the setting you want to disable. For example, you may only want to allow team owners to be able to add and remove apps so you can uncheck the option Allow members to add and remove apps.

FIGURE 2.42
Member Permissions

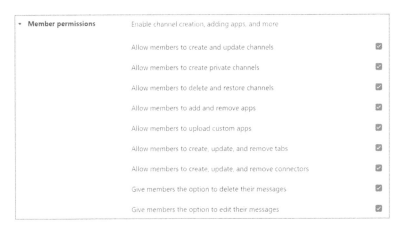

Guest Permissions

Guest Permissions for a team are for enabling guests (users outside your organizations) to create, update, and delete channels. These settings are turned off by default, and it's rare to enable this setting for your guest users (see Figure 2.43).

FIGURE 2.43
Guest Permissions

@mentions

The @mentions settings are for choosing who can use @team and @channel mentions within the team. These settings are enabled by default (see Figure 2.44).

FIGURE 2.44
@mentions settings

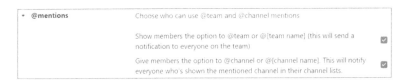

Team Code

Team Code provides the ability to generate a code so people can join the team directly without getting join requests. To allow people to join with a code you first need to Generate a code for the team, then you can distribute the code which others can input into the text box to Join a team with a code (see Figure 2.45).

FIGURE 2.45
Team Code generation

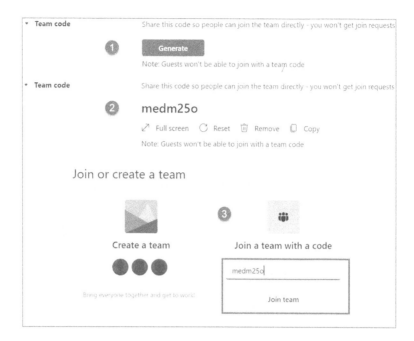

Fun Stuff

Fun Stuff includes settings for enabling/disabling emoji, memes, GIFs, and stickers in conversations (see Figure 2.46). By default these settings are enabled which gives people the ability to add a giphy (see Figure 2.47) or a sticker/meme (see Figure 2.48) to a conversation. You can disable and reenable for your team anytime. If you disable your team the icons in the chat will no longer appear (see Figure 2.49).

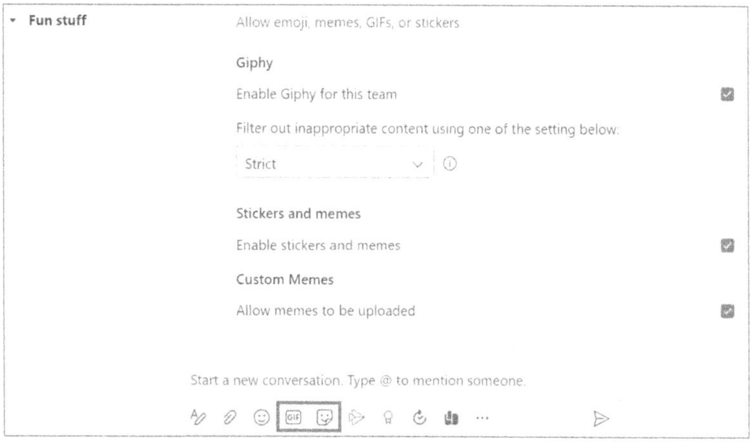

FIGURE 2.46
Fun Stuff settings

FIGURE 2.47
Giphy feature in
chat message

FIGURE 2.48
Stickers and Meme
feature in chat message

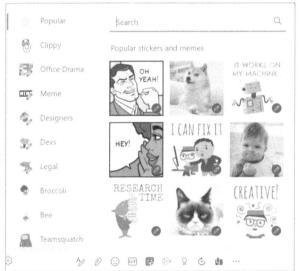

FIGURE 2.49
Giphy, Stickers and
Meme feature disabled

Tags

The Tags setting is where team owners can choose who can manage tags. The default setting is set to Team Owners, but you can change the settings to allow Team Owners And Members (see Figure 2.50). Tags provide the ability for you to categorize people based on attributes such as project, role, or location. To create a tag you simply navigate to the Tags tab and then click on Create tag (see Figure 2.51 and Figure 2.52). For example, you can set up a tag for grouping your Production Managers that are members of your team (see Figure 2.53).

FIGURE 2.50
Tags settings

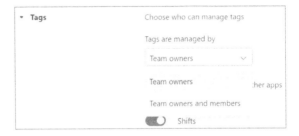

FIGURE 2.51
Tags tab for creating and managing tags in team

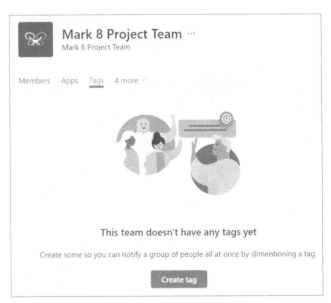

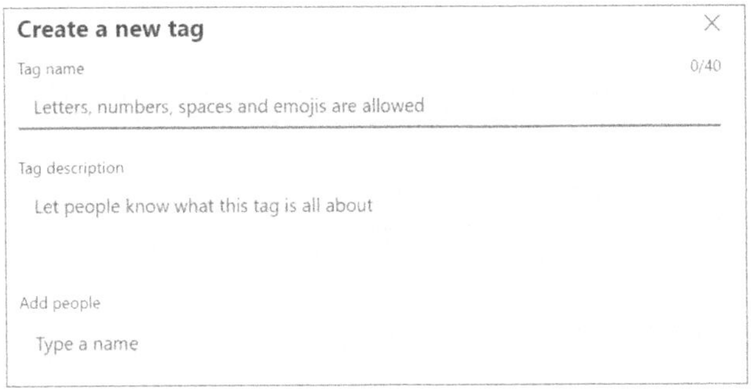

FIGURE 2.52
Create new tag dialog

FIGURE 2.53
Production Managers
tag example

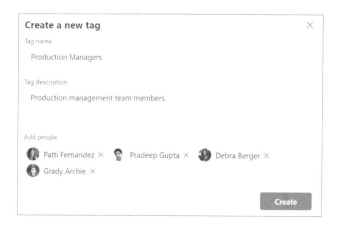

Once the tag is created, you will see it listed on your tags page (see Figure 2.54). You can click on the tag to modify the tag name or add or remove people from the tag (see Figure 2.55). The benefit of using tags is so you can mention them in a conversation without having to type each person's name (see Figure 2.56). You can easily see more details of the tag by hovering over the name with your cursor which opens a panel showing more details of the tag. From there you can click on Chat with group (see Figure 2.57) to start a group chat with the members of the tag (see Figure 2.58).

FIGURE 2.54
Tags tab showing newly
created tag for
Production Managers

FIGURE 2.55
Editing Production
Managers tag

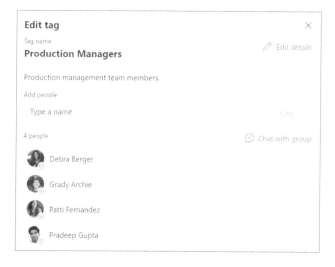

FIGURE 2.56
Using tag in
conversation

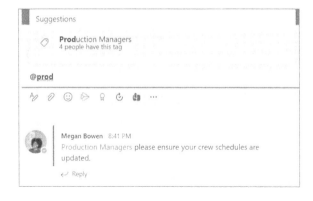

FIGURE 2.57
Details pane when you
hover over tag mention

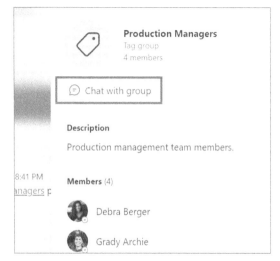

FIGURE 2.58
Group chat started from
Production
Managers tag

ANALYTICS

The Analytics tab in the Manage team settings is where team owners can view per-team analytics (see Figure 2.59). This information gives insight into usage patterns and activity on teams you have access to or manage.

FIGURE 2.59
Teams analytics

The analytics include the following:

Summary

Users

Total number of users in a specified time period (this includes team owners, team members, and guests).

Posts

Number of new messages posted in the team chat during specified time period.

Replies

Number of replies in a team chat during specified time period.

Apps

Number of apps added to the team.

Meetings

Number of Teams meetings organized at the team level.

Active users

Number of active and inactive users.

Role

Number of users by role (this includes team owners, team members, and guests).

Active users chart

Chart of number of daily active users. Hovering over the dot on a given date will display the number of active users for that date.

Members chart

Chart of total number of messages posted in a team chat by date.

APPS

The Apps tab is where team owners can see the list of apps installed for the team as being able to delete and add more apps (see Figure 2.60).

FIGURE 2.60
Apps settings for team

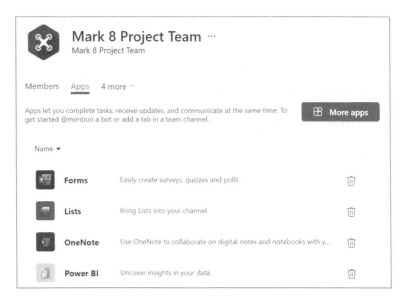

DELETE A TEAM

By default, team owners can delete teams of which they are an owner. When you choose to delete a team, a dialog will be displayed with a confirmation message and a check box to confirm you understand that everything will be deleted. Once you check the box, the Delete Team button becomes enabled so you can proceed with the deletion (see Figure 2.61).

FIGURE 2.61
Deleting a team

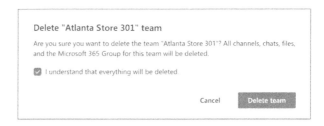

Delete "Atlanta Store 301" team

Are you sure you want to delete the team "Atlanta Store 301"? All channels, chats, files, and the Microsoft 365 Group for this team will be deleted.

☑ I understand that everything will be deleted.

Cancel   **Delete team**

ARCHIVE A TEAM

Another option you have in Teams is to archive a team. A common scenario is when an organization is using Teams to manage projects. When a project ends, you may want to keep the team as a reference or just in case you need to reactivate it in the future. When you archive a team, the conversations and files in the team become read-only. Search is still available for an archived team, and it can also be saved as a favorite. Only Teams administrators can archive teams through the Microsoft Teams admin center.

NOTE   To learn more about archiving and restoring a team,
please visit `https://support.microsoft.com/en-us/office/`
`archive-or-restore-a-team-dc161cfd-b328-440f-974b-5da5bd98b5a7`.

Best Practices

As more organizations are continuing to roll out Teams, there are some recommendations for companies that have large teams and recommendations on how to roll out Teams for better user adoption.

MANAGING LARGE TEAMS

Many organizations create teams to facilitate communications between small groups of people. However, there are scenarios where large teams are needed. Some example scenarios include large teams for department-wide collaboration, collaboration in employee resource groups, and collaboration between internal and external members. While Teams is equally effective in facilitating communications between large teams, the increase in team size can lead to unique management and operational challenges.

Some recommendations for large teams include:

◆ Create channels to focus on discussions.

◆ Restrict channel creation for team members (see Figure 2.62).

◆ Set channels you want to show by default for members (see Figure 2.63).

◆ Regulate application and bots in large teams (see Figure 2.64).

◆ Regulate team and channel mentions. While team and channel mentions are great to draw the attention of the whole team to a certain channel post, this is not recommended for large teams. Once a mention is used in a post, a notification is sent to all team members and this can overload the thousands of members in a large team. You can turn this setting off in the @mentions settings for the team (see Figure 2.65).

FIGURE 2.62
Restricting channel permissions

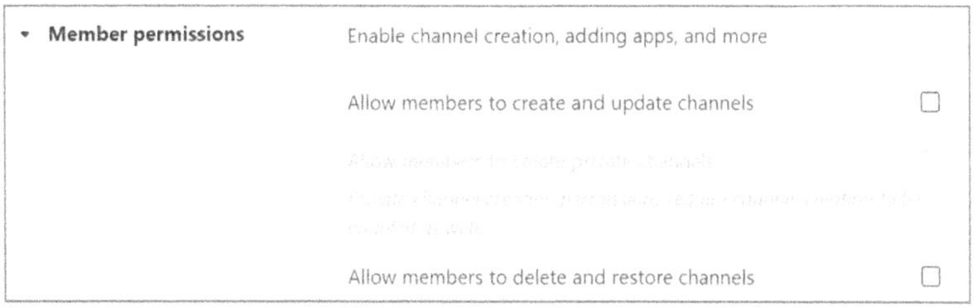

Member permissions	Enable channel creation, adding apps, and more	
	Allow members to create and update channels	☐
	Allow members to delete and restore channels	☐

FIGURE 2.63
Showing/hiding channels by default for members

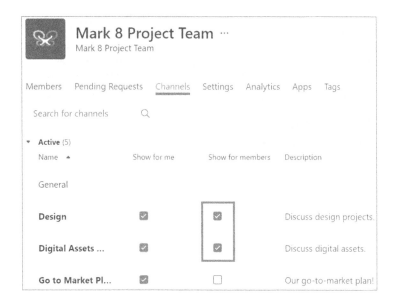

FIGURE 2.64
Enabling/disabling apps and connectors

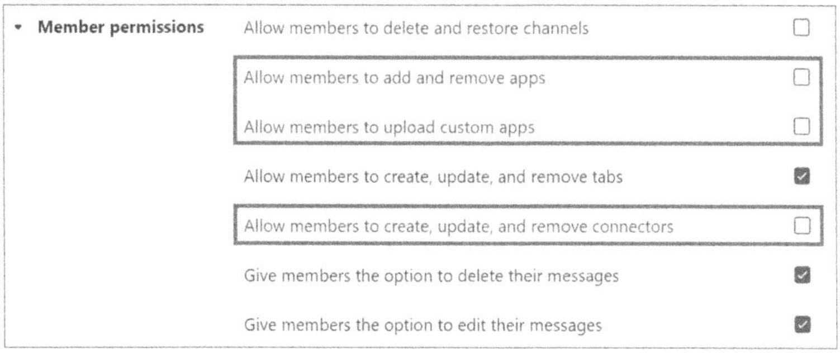

Member permissions	Allow members to delete and restore channels	☐
	Allow members to add and remove apps	☐
	Allow members to upload custom apps	☐
	Allow members to create, update, and remove tabs	☑
	Allow members to create, update, and remove connectors	☐
	Give members the option to delete their messages	☑
	Give members the option to edit their messages	☑

FIGURE 2.65
Enabling/disabling
@mention notifications

ADDING TEAMS GRADUALLY

When you first roll out Teams, it is recommended you start with a small number of teams and team members, and then gradually add new people or groups as you go. They will be able to quickly catch up on discussions since conversations and files are available to users regardless of when they join. Doing a gradual rollout will help with user adoption. Another recommendation is to avoid creating a bunch of teams with the same set of members. Instead, create channels in a single team, which brings us to the next topic of creating channels to focus on discussions.

NAMING POLICY

Since Teams is backed by Microsoft 365 groups, you can use a group naming policy to enforce a consistent naming strategy. The naming policy provides you with the ability to choose a naming convention for your Microsoft 365 group and Teams workspaces to standardize how the assets are named. While every organization is different, there is no one size fits all; however, here are some examples (see Figure 2.66) that can be implemented:

Project Teams – [PRJ]-[Descriptive Name]

Guest Access Enabled Teams – [EXT or GUEST]-[Descriptive Name]

Multi-national Teams Example – [Geography]-[Business Unit]-[Descriptive Name]

FIGURE 2.66
Teams using example
naming policy

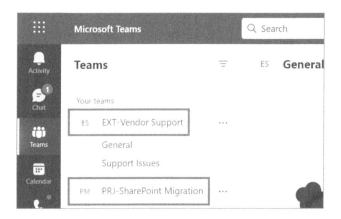

NOTE To read more about Microsoft 365 groups naming policy, please visit
`https://docs.microsoft.com/en-us/microsoft-365/solutions/`
`groups-naming-policy?view=o365-worldwide`.

Working with Channels

Channels are one of the core features of Teams, and it is important to understand how to manage them within a team.

Creating Channels

Channels are easy to create in Teams. Simply click on the three dots for the team and select Add channel, then fill out the name, description (optional), and choose if the channel will be Standard or Private (see Figure 2.67). Creating a standard channel will automatically make it accessible to everyone on the team. When you create a private channel, you will be prompted to add members to the channel (see Figure 2.68).

FIGURE 2.67
Creating a new channel
for a team

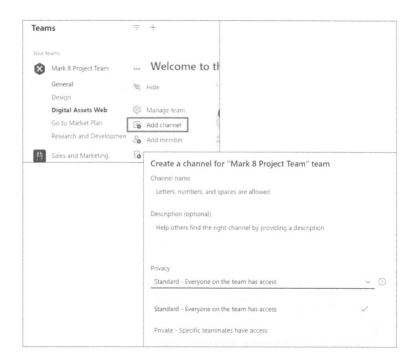

Channel Moderation

For standard channels, team owners can turn on moderation to control who can start new posts and reply to posts (see Figure 2.69). What can a channel moderator do?

◆ Start new posts in the channel:

  ◆ Moderators can start new posts in the channel and control whether team members can reply to existing channel messages.

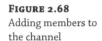

FIGURE 2.68
Adding members to
the channel

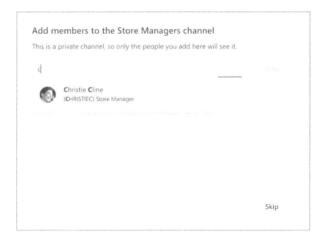

◆ Add and remove team members as moderators to a channel:

   ◆ Team owners can assign moderators within a channel. (By default, team owners are channel moderators and can't be removed.)

   ◆ Moderators within a channel can add or remove other moderators within the channel.

◆ Control whether:

   ◆ Team members can reply to existing channel messages.

   ◆ Bots and connectors can submit channel messages.

Sending Messages in a Channel

To start a new conversation in a channel, go to the Posts tab of the channel you want to send a message to and click the New Conversation button (see Figure 2.70). This will open the compose message box where you can type and send your message, or you can click the Format icon under the box to expand the formatting toolbar (see Figure 2.71).

Sending Announcements in a Channel

Sometimes your messages need to stand out more than a regular conversation. Channel messages provide an option to send an announcement with a headline and image. To compose an announcement, click the Format icon in the compose box. At the top of the box that appears, click the arrow next to New Conversation > Announcement (see Figure 2.72). The compose box will update with options for a headline, subhead, and message body. You can change the color of the headline or add an image by clicking the color or image icon (see Figure 2.73).

FIGURE 2.69
Channel permissions

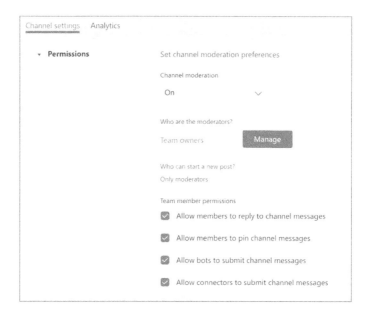

FIGURE 2.70
New conversation

FIGURE 2.71
Format icon

FIGURE 2.72
Creating an
Announcement message

FIGURE 2.73
Announcement
formatting options

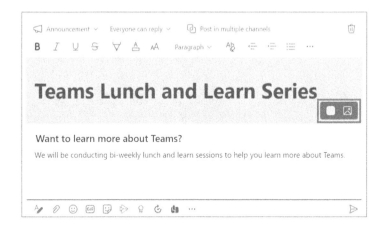

NOTE Announcement messages are available only in channels and are not available in 1:1 or group chats.

Cross-Post a Channel Conversation

Do you have an announcement or information that needs to be shared across multiple teams and channels? If so, you can post a message to multiple channels at once. To do this, click Post In Multiple Channels and then click the Select Channels button (see Figure 2.74). You will be prompted with a Choose Channels dialog where you can choose all the channels you want to post the message to (see Figure 2.75). Once you choose the channels and click Update, the dialog will close and the compose message box will have the To field updated with all the channels you selected (see Figure 2.76). Once you click the send icon to post you will be able to see your announcements posted in the multiple channels you selected. Cross-Post channel messages will have a chain icon (see Figure 2.77). You can edit the channel message anytime which will update to all the locations it's been posted in, and you can also remove it from other channels by editing the message, removing the channels you don't want, and then click the check mark icon (see Figure 2.78).

FIGURE 2.74
Posting an announcement to multiple channels

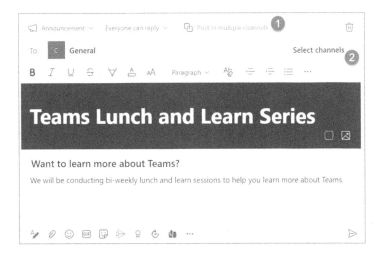

Best Practices

Channels are a great way to separate conversations around topics, and there are some recommended best practices for creating channels and use of the General channel.

CREATE CHANNELS TO FOCUS ON DISCUSSIONS

As mentioned earlier in this chapter, the purpose of channels is to help keep conversations organized. The best practice recommendation is to use channels to focus on discussions instead of creating large amounts of teams.

FIGURE 2.75
Choose Channels dialog

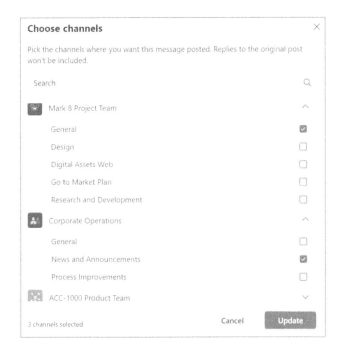

FIGURE 2.76
Preview of
Announcement
with channels

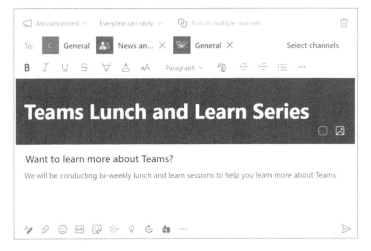

FIGURE 2.77
Posted channel message
example with
chain link icon

FIGURE 2.78
Removing post from
channel example with
check mark icon

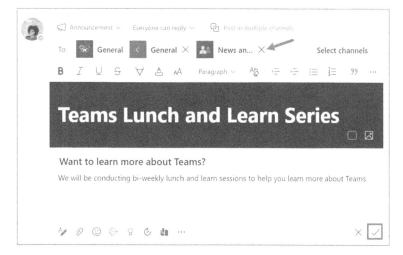

USING THE GENERAL CHANNEL

When a team is created from scratch, it includes a General channel. You can't remove, rename, or unfavorite the General channel, but you can change the settings. The General channel can become quite noisy, especially when the default setting allows all team members to post to it. To eliminate noise, the best practice recommendation is to only allow team owners to post to the General channel. To change the setting:

◆ Go to the General channel and click the three dots ⋯ More Options ➤ Manage Channel (see Figure 2.79).

◆ Under the General Channel section of the Channel settings tab, select Only Owners Can Post Messages (see Figure 2.80).

FIGURE 2.79
Manage Channel link

FIGURE 2.79
Manage Channel link

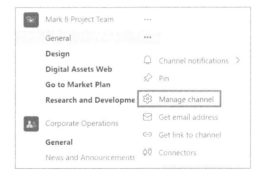

FIGURE 2.80
Setting to only allow
owners to post messages
in the General channel

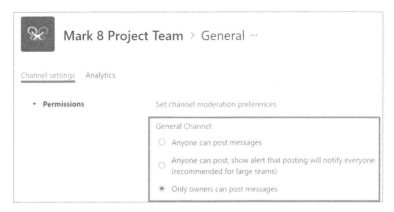

Teams Templates

As mentioned earlier in this chapter, you can create a team from scratch or from an existing group or team. In addition to that you can create teams from a template. Microsoft Teams has predefined team templates available by default within your tenant. Each template is a predefined set of channels, tabs, and apps around a business or project need. When you create a team, you'll see a Select From A Template section where you can choose from a growing library of templates to help you set up a team quickly and easily (see Figure 2.81). You may have a need to use a prebuilt template for projects. For example, the Manage A Project template includes 4 channels and 4 apps (see Figure 2.82).

To create a team from a Teams template, click Join Or Create A Team and choose the Create A Team tile (see Figure 2.83). Under Select From A Template, scroll and select the desired template (see Figure 2.84). After you select the desired template, the dialog will display the predefined channels and apps; to create, click Next (see Figure 2.85).

After you click Next, the dialog will ask if you want to create the team as private or public (see Figure 2.86). Next, give your new team a name and click Create (see Figure 2.87). Teams will then proceed with creating the new team (see Figure 2.88). The new team is created with the predefined channels (see Figure 2.89).

FIGURE 2.81
Select from a template
dialog screen

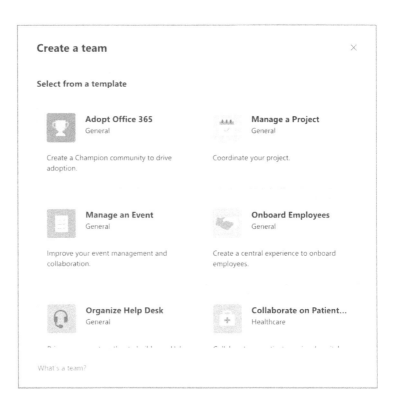

FIGURE 2.82
Displaying contents of
the Manage a
Project template

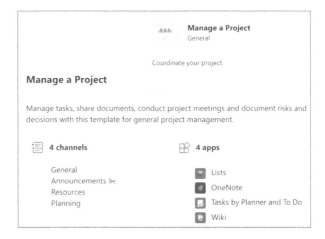

FIGURE 2.83
Join or create a team
link and Create team tile

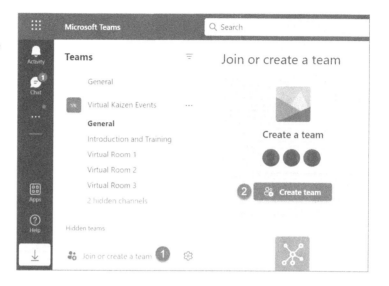

FIGURE 2.84
Selecting the Manage a
Project example

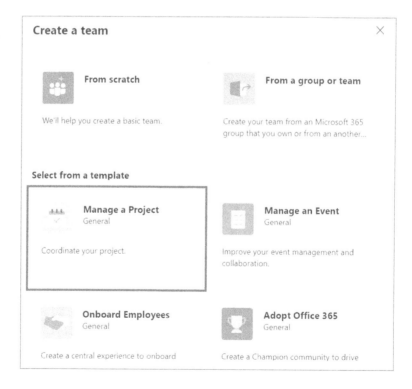

FIGURE 2.85
Click Next to
build your team

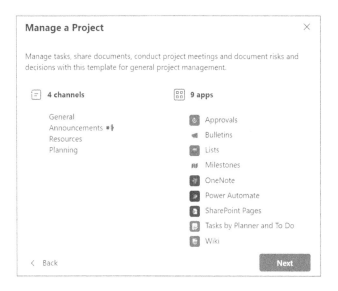

FIGURE 2.86
Private or Public team
permission option

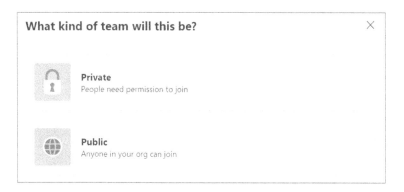

FIGURE 2.87
Naming your new team

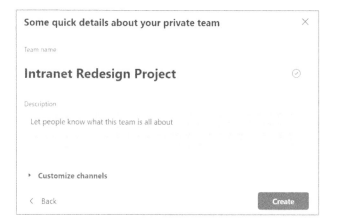

FIGURE 2.88
Creating The Team
process dialog

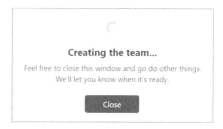

FIGURE 2.89
New team created

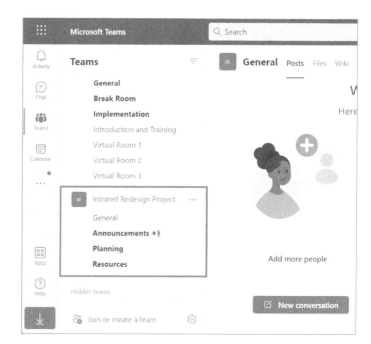

User Presence in Microsoft Teams

Presence is part of a user's profile in Teams that indicates the user's current availability and status to other users. A user's presence is updated in real-time on the web, mobile, and desktop version of Teams. By default, any user within your organization can see your online presence, and your presence will automatically update unless you override your status manually. For example, if you are away for a period of time your status will change to "Away" and will reset automatically when you return.

Status Duration Setting

One of the features in Teams I use frequently is the ability to set my online presence status for a duration of time. For example, I might be online after work hours and want my Teams status to show "Away." There are times I've done this and have forgotten to reset my status. Then I join a Teams call and realize I'm still showing away, and which I then reset my status manually. Or I've set my status to "Busy" or "Do not disturb" and forgot to reset it after I was done. Thankfully, this is no longer an issue. Anytime I want to temporarily change my status, I set my status for a duration of time, and then it automatically resets after the time is up. To change, you simply click on the drop-down menu for your status in Teams and choose Duration (see Figure 2.90). Then set your status and time frame (see Figure 2.91).

FIGURE 2.90
Duration menu option when manually changing online presence status

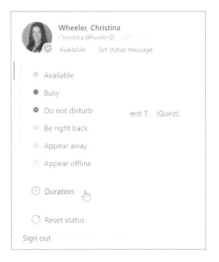

FIGURE 2.91
Example showing duration being set to a custom time frame

NOTE There could be times where your actual presence status isn't reflecting correctly in Teams. This is a known issue that Microsoft has documented workarounds for. To read about this issue and how to resolve, please visit https://docs.microsoft.com/en-us/microsoftteams/troubleshoot/teams-im-presence/presence-not-show-actual-status.

The Bottom Line

Teams and channels.   The Teams workspace owners are empowered to manage their teams and channels in a manner that they envision. It is very important for them to manage the channels in a way that makes sense for the needs of the team members.

> **Master It**   The training department has a request to organize, collaborate, and share existing files, and they have a need to create new files as part of their quarterly training assessments. They would like to use Microsoft Teams to manage their assessments, but they don't know how to organize channels. Currently, all their files are stored on a file share and they email updates back and forth with each other to collaborate.

Team membership and roles.   The team membership and roles are defined by the Office 365 group created with the team. The team owner will need to decide who will be co-owner and who will be members of the team. The team owner will need to identify and assign users to contribute or assist with managing the team.

> **Master It**   You need to allow members of your team to add additional members for a new project. This will assist you with making sure the right members on the team are added in a timely manner without you being the bottleneck.

Managing teams.   As an IT admin, one important task is understanding the life-cycle management of teams. As a team owner the life-cycle management goes beyond the administration controls and gets more involved with understanding the life cycle of content.

> **Master It**   You are the team owner and have been asked to start planning the retirement of a team used for the latest completed project. You have been requested to retain the content and keep the team available for reference if needed. You will need to retain the team for 7 years.

Working with channels.   The channel feature provides a way for teams to be organized and structured by topics or common interests. The team owner can empower members of the team to manage specific channel components or sharing capabilities.

> **Master It**   You have a few channels on your team for which you don't have the subject matter expertise at the channel level. You have several team members that do have the subject matter expertise at the channel level to best support channel moderation.

Teams templates.   The teams template feature in Microsoft Teams provides flexibility for the IT admin and organization on whether they want to start with a predefined teams template or create one from scratch.

> **Master It**   You have built a team structure with specific channels, tabs, and apps that provided value to a project team. You have been tasked with replicating that team for all projects for the future using Teams.

Chapter 3

Meetings and Conferencing

Microsoft Teams is more than just chat and collaboration. While you can have quick conversations in Teams, there's so much more to it. With Teams you can easily schedule meetings, live events, and webinars where attendees can join from anywhere using the Teams desktop app, mobile app, or browser.

IN THIS CHAPTER, YOU WILL LEARN THE FOLLOWING

- ◆ Understanding meetings in Teams
- ◆ Understanding calls in Teams
- ◆ Live events and webinars
- ◆ Breakout rooms
- ◆ Audio conferencing in Teams

Overview of Meetings and Conferencing

There are three different ways to meet in Teams:

- ◆ **Meetings**: Meetings in Teams include audio, video, and screen sharing for up to 1,000 people. Anyone can join a Teams meeting without having to be a member of the organization or needing to have a Teams account.

- ◆ **Live events**: Live events are an extension of Teams meetings that enable you to schedule and produce events that stream to large audiences of up to 10,000 people.

- ◆ **Webinars**: You can host webinars with up to 1,000 participants using Teams. Presenters can share audio, video, and content. Attendees can engage in webinars through reactions, chat, and answering poll questions. Attendees cannot share their own audio, video, or content.

NOTE   For the latest meetings and calls limitations in Microsoft Teams, please visit https://docs.microsoft.com/en-us/microsoftteams/ limits-specifications-teams#meetings-and-calls.

Meetings and Conferencing Prerequisites

Anyone can attend a Teams meeting, webinar, or live event for free as licenses are not required for attendees. On the other hand, people who need to organize, schedule, and host meetings or live events do need a license. If you are already using Teams within your organization, it's most likely you already have a license. If you don't have one and want to organize and host meetings or live events, you'll need a Microsoft 365 or Office 365 license.

NOTE For more details on Microsoft Teams add-on licenses, please visit `https://docs` `.microsoft.com/en-us/MicrosoftTeams/teams-add-on-licensing/` `microsoft-teams-add-on-licensing?tabs=small-business.`

Meetings in Teams

With more and more people working from home, having the ability to meet virtually has become extremely important. No matter where you are, you can meet with others in Teams using audio, video, chat, and screen sharing. Teams meetings has become one of the core ways people are collaborating inside and outside the organization all around the world.

Private Meetings vs. Channel Meetings

You can create two types of meetings in Teams: private meetings and channel meetings. Private meetings are invites sent from within Outlook or Teams tied to a personal or organizational account. If you are used to creating meeting invites in Outlook or other email tools, then you are already familiar with private meetings. Private meetings are where you create an invite and add required and optional attendees through email addresses. When an attendee accepts the invite of a private meeting, the event gets added to their calendar.

Channel meetings are different in that they are scheduled from within Teams. When you schedule a channel meeting, anyone in the team can join. You can schedule a channel meeting directly within a team channel using the Meet drop-down (see Figure 3.1) or by adding the channel (see Figure 3.2) to the invite created from within the calendar in Teams.

FIGURE 3.1
Channel example showing drop-down menu to schedule a meeting

In the following example, a channel meeting is being created in the Leadership channel of the Mark 8 Project Team. The channel meeting is set up as a recurring meeting every 2 weeks (see Figure 3.3).

FIGURE 3.2
List of channels showing
under the Add
Channel text box

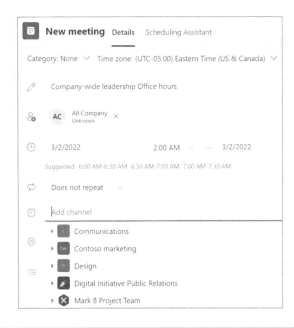

FIGURE 3.3
Recurring channel
meeting invite draft

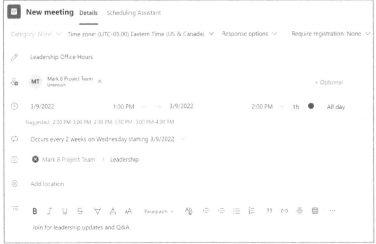

You can invite individual people or groups. If you invite a group, all members of the group will receive a meeting invite in their email account (see Figure 3.4). If accepted, the channel meeting will get added to their personal calendar (see Figure 3.5). Channel meetings will show in the channel they were scheduled in and anyone in the team can join the meeting (see Figure 3.6).

FIGURE 3.4
Channel meeting
email invite

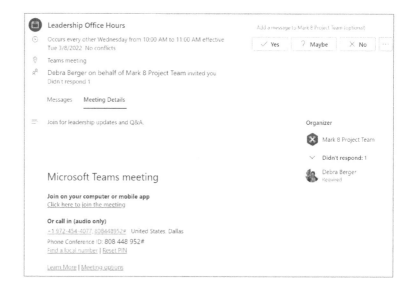

FIGURE 3.5
Accepted channel
meeting shown in
Outlook personal
calendar

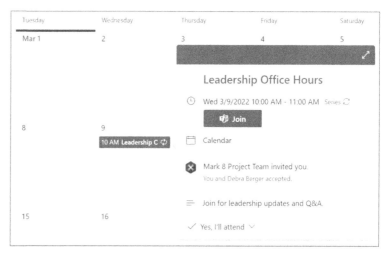

The functionality of a channel meeting is similar to a standard Teams meeting, but you should be aware of several key differences (see Figure 3.7):

Chat

Standard meeting: Anyone in the meeting can use the meeting chat. The meeting chat will show in each person's "Chat" area of Teams.

Channel meeting: Since the channel meeting happens within a team, only people in the team will be able to use or view the chat. Other users will get a message "Only team members can chat. Ask the team owner to make you a member."

FIGURE 3.6
Channel meeting posted
in a team chat

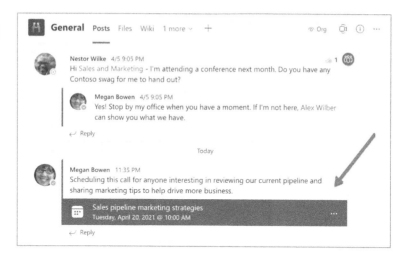

Recording

Standard meeting: The recording will be posted in the meeting chat and the recording file is stored in the organizer's OneDrive for Business. All the attendees can access the recording and the sharing permissions to the recording are applied automatically.

Channel meeting: Only members in the team will have access to the recording. They can view it from SharePoint or the meeting chat (see Figure 3.7). People who are not in the team cannot view it from chat or SharePoint, but the owner of the recording can grant the non-team members permissions to view the recording.

Scheduling

Standard meeting: Can be scheduled from within Outlook or in Teams.

Channel meeting: Can only be scheduled from within Teams.

FIGURE 3.7
Channel meeting
recording showing
in chat

Scheduling a Meeting

You can schedule meetings in many ways, and since your calendar in Teams is connected to your Exchange calendar, any time you schedule a meeting within Teams it will show up in Outlook and vice versa.

SCHEDULE A MEETING IN OUTLOOK

When you schedule a meeting in Outlook (web or client), you will have a Teams meeting option you can choose when scheduling or editing a meeting invite (see Figure 3.8). The Scheduling Assistant is a common feature people use in Outlook when scheduling meetings, especially when scheduling with people within your organization (see Figure 3.9).

FIGURE 3.8
Teams meeting option in Outlook web client meeting invite

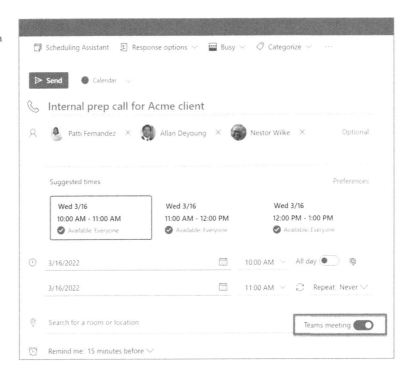

SCHEDULE A MEETING IN TEAMS

You can schedule a meeting directly in the Teams app by going to your calendar in Teams and then clicking + New Meeting or selecting Schedule Meeting from the drop-down menu (see Figure 3.10). When you create a new meeting in Teams it will default to the Details pane where you can set the details, add attendees, set the date/time, recurrence, add to a channel, add a location, and provide additional details about the meeting (see Figure 3.11).

FIGURE 3.9
Outlook
Scheduling Assistant

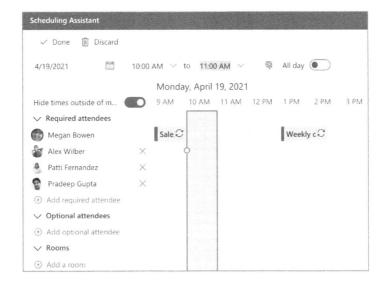

FIGURE 3.10
New Meeting drop-down
in Teams app

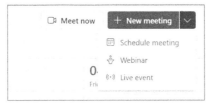

FIGURE 3.11
New Teams meeting
Details pane

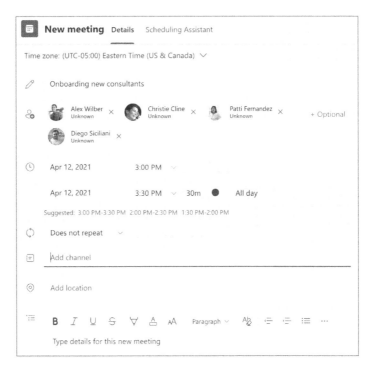

If you are adding attendees within your organization, you can see their availability through the Scheduling Assistant pane (see Figure 3.12). You will not see the profile details of attendees being added outside of your organization, and sometimes attendees within your organization may not show up at times either. Teams will provide suggested times based on availability below the date and time options (see Figure 3.13). The suggested times are based on availability of the organizer, and anyone being invited can see their schedule.

FIGURE 3.12
Teams
Scheduling Assistant

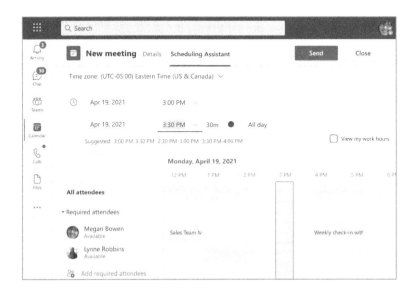

FIGURE 3.13
Scheduling Assistant
showing time zone and
date options with
suggested times

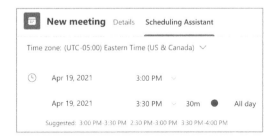

TEAMS MEETING OPTIONS

When you schedule a Teams meeting it will have default settings applied, which you can change at any time before the meeting. To access the meeting options of a scheduled meeting the location depends on if you're editing the meeting in Teams or Outlook. When editing from Teams web or Teams client you should see a Meetings Options link you can click (see Figure 3.14).

If you're editing a meeting in Outlook web, you will see a Meeting Options link in the auto-generated Teams meeting details (see Figure 3.15). When you click the link it will launch the settings in the browser. Some of the options you can set include who can bypass the lobby, whether to announce when callers enter or leave the meeting, who can present, whether to allow attendees to use their mic and camera, and whether to allow meeting chat and reactions (see Figure 3.16).

FIGURE 3.14
Meeting Options
link in Teams

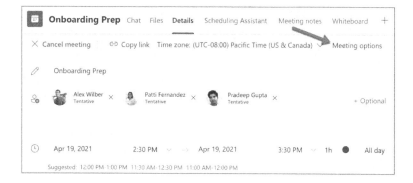

FIGURE 3.15
Meeting Options link in
Outlook web

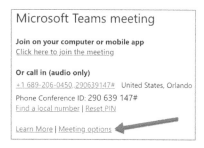

FIGURE 3.16
Teams meeting options
default settings

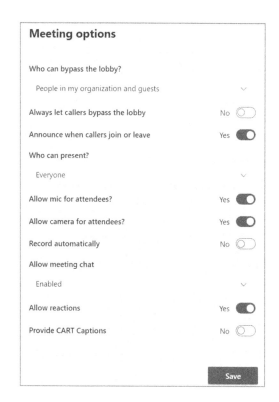

Bypass Lobby Settings

By default, when a Teams meeting is scheduled the meeting does not allow callers to bypass the lobby. The default setting for Who Can Bypass The Lobby? is People In My Organization And Guests. You can change this setting by selecting another option in the drop-down (see Figure 3.17). If you have a need to always let callers bypass the lobby, you can set the toggle to Yes.

FIGURE 3.17
Who Can Bypass The
Lobby? choices

Who Can Present

Another default setting you may want to change for your meetings is who you want to allow to present in the meeting. The default is Everyone, but you can change this setting to be more specific (see Figure 3.18).

FIGURE 3.18
Who Can
Present? choices

Allowing Attendees to Use Mic and Camera

There could be a situation in which you do not want to allow attendees to use their mic or camera. If you need to, you can disable both options by setting the Allow Mic For Attendees and Allow Camera For Attendees toggle.

Allow Meeting Chat

Meeting chat is enabled by default, but you can disable this or set it to allow chat for In-Meeting Only (see Figure 3.19). In-meeting means the chat will be available during the meeting but will not be available before and after the meeting. If you want chat to be available for this meeting before, during, and after, then leave this setting set to Enabled.

FIGURE 3.19
Allow Meeting
Chat choices

Allow Reactions

The last setting option you can change for your meeting is allowing or disallowing reactions. Reactions are when a user can respond to a message in a meeting chat with an emoji. Disabling this feature will block users from being able to do that.

START AN INSTANT MEETING

Another option you have instead of scheduling a meeting is to start an impromptu instant meeting. You can start an instant meeting by going to the Calendar in Teams and clicking Meet Now. A dialog box will appear where you can rename the instant meeting, get a link to share, or proceed with starting the meeting (see Figure 3.20).

FIGURE 3.20
Meet Now meeting
dialog box options

Joining a Meeting

When you create a Teams meeting it generates a link for yourself and anyone you invite to join (see Figure 3.21). Attendees can join a Teams meeting via a mobile device, tablet, computer using the Teams client, or through a browser.

FIGURE 3.21
Teams meeting link and
audio conference
example

JOIN FROM CALENDAR

In addition to using the link in the invite, attendees can join a Teams meeting using the Join button in the calendar event in Teams (see Figure 3.22) or in Outlook on the web (see Figure 3.23).

FIGURE 3.22
Join Teams meeting through button in Teams

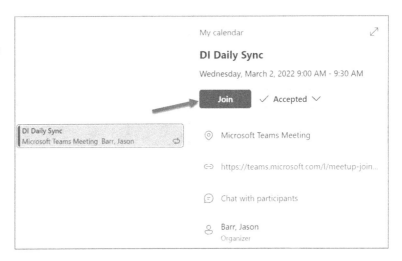

FIGURE 3.23
Join Teams meeting through the Join button in Outlook on the web

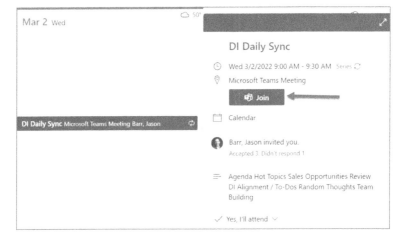

JOIN MEETINGS IN A CHANNEL OR CHAT

If a meeting takes place in a channel, you'll see an invitation to join, relevant content, and who is in the meeting right in the channel. You can easily join the meeting by clicking the invite in the channel (see Figure 3.24). You can click + Add To Calendar to accept the invite or, if the channel meeting is in session, simply click the Join button or the Click Here To Join The Meeting link (see Figure 3.25). If a meeting you have been invited to has already begun, it will appear in your recent chat list. You can join by selecting the meeting in your chat list and then clicking Join at the top of the chat.

FIGURE 3.24
Meeting invite in
Teams channel

FIGURE 3.25
The Join button and the
Click Here To Join The
Meeting link

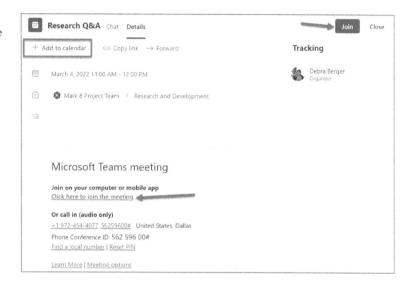

CALL IN

Not all Teams meetings provide a phone number to call in. Having a phone number of a Teams
meeting is dependent on the invite being sent out by an account that has the audio conferencing
add-on enabled. If there is a phone number available, you can join meetings by calling the phone
number listed in the invite (see Figure 3.26). We'll cover more details about the ability to call in
later in this chapter when we discuss audio conferencing.

FIGURE 3.26
Call in meeting info

ADD A ROOM WHILE YOU JOIN

If you have a meeting room set up or are using a device such as a Microsoft Surface Hub 2S, you can add a room while you join a meeting. Personal Bluetooth devices can also be used, which may get detected as a room when you join. When you join a meeting and choose your audio and video settings, you'll have an option to add a room so you can use the meeting room's audio and video devices. If there are meeting rooms nearby (see Figure 3.27) or supported personal Bluetooth devices, you'll see the meeting room's name and the option to Join And Add This Room. If the nearby room has already joined the meeting, you can Join with audio off to avoid disrupting the meeting.

FIGURE 3.27
Join And Add This
Room option

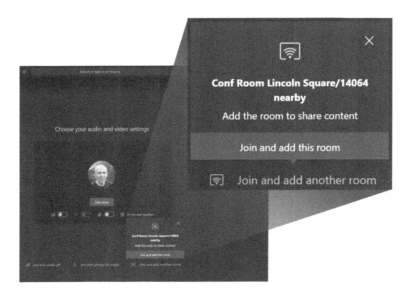

JOINING A MEETING ON A SECOND DEVICE

When you join a meeting on one device, you have the option to join from another one at the same time (see Figure 3.28). Joining from another device can come in handy, especially if you're in a meeting on your phone but there's content on your laptop you'd like to share or vice versa. You can transfer the meeting to the other device or keep both devices in the meeting by adding the second device (see Figure 3.29). To prevent an echo effect, Teams will automatically mute the mic on your second device before it enters the meeting. Once it's joined, you will be able to turn the mic and camera on or off as needed. With both devices in the meeting, you can share content from either device.

FIGURE 3.28
Joining from
another device

FIGURE 3.29
Add This Device and
Transfer To This
Device options

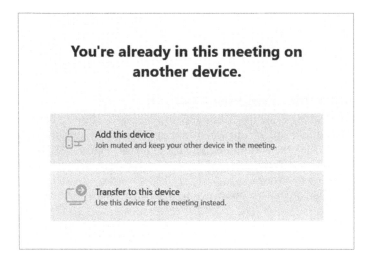

Using Video in Microsoft Teams

Using video for Teams meetings has become a common practice for many organizations. For example, at Core BTS it is highly encouraged that everyone within the organization is on camera in meetings. While it's not required at Core BTS, it is recommended especially when meeting with clients. Whether you use video for meetings or not, the great thing is that there are many ways to customize your video experience when you join a Teams meeting or call. Some settings will vary depending on whether you are joining a Teams meeting or call using the desktop client, web browser, tablet, or mobile device.

TURN YOUR VIDEO ON OR OFF

Teams allows you to share your video any time when you join a meeting from a device with a camera. Before you join a meeting, you can decide to enable or disable your video simply by clicking the Video toggle (see Figure 3.30). There are times during a meeting when you may want to turn your video on and off throughout the course of the meeting. For example, you may only want people to see your video when you're talking but turn it off when others are talking. This can be helpful especially when the meeting has a large number of participants, such as community calls. To turn the camera on and off, go to the meeting controls any time during the meeting and tap the camera icon (see Figure 3.31).

FIGURE 3.30
Disabling your video
before a meeting

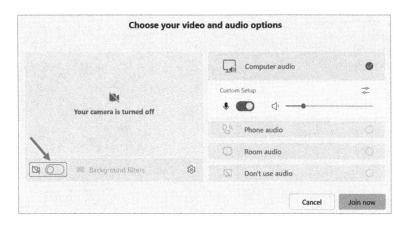

FIGURE 3.31
Turning off video
during a meeting

FIGURE 3.31
Turning off video
during a meeting

CHANGE YOUR VIDEO BACKGROUND

If you're calling using the Teams app on a mobile device or computer, you can change what appears behind you in your video. You can blur the background or replace the background with an image using the Background Filters option (see Figure 3.32 and Figure 3.33). Using background filters has become a highly adopted feature, especially with those working from home and needing to be on camera during calls. Teams provides default backgrounds that you can choose from, or you can upload your own by clicking + Add New (see Figure 3.34).

FIGURE 3.32
Background
Filters option

FIGURE 3.33
Teams video blur
background settings

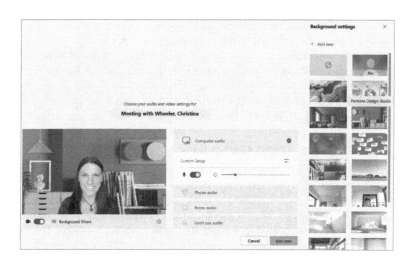

FIGURE 3.34
Teams Add New link for
uploading your own
custom back-
ground image

NOTE   If you don't see the option to turn on background effects, this means the feature is not available on the device you're joining from. Background effects is available through the Teams app (mobile or computer) and when joining from a web browser.

For more details about customizing your background, please visit `www.microsoft.com/ microsoft-teams/background-blur?ocid=oo_support_mix_marvel_ups_support_ smcteam_inline`.

For additional virtual backgrounds Microsoft has made available online to download for free, please visit `www.microsoft.com/en-us/microsoft-teams/ virtual-meeting-backgrounds#office-ContentAreaHeadingTemplate-r1sx4yv`.

CHOOSE A VIDEO LAYOUT

When you join a Teams meeting on the desktop or mobile app, the meeting will default to a Gallery view showing video streams of up to nine other people on your screen at the same time (see Figure 3.35). You can choose from several different video layouts during the meeting. The options available depend on the size of the meeting, where you are joining from (app versus browser), and the number of people you'd like to see on your screen at once.

FIGURE 3.35
Meeting window
showing nine different
video streams at once

Gallery

The Gallery view is the default view when you join a meeting on desktop or mobile. If there are more than nine attendees in the meeting, Teams will prioritize the people who have their video turned on, as well as those who are speaking the most. For those who haven't turned on their video, Teams will show their profile pic or initials if they do not have a pic.

Large Gallery

The Large gallery view enables you to see the videos of up to 49 other people at once (see Figure 3.36). This option becomes available when there are at least ten people in the meeting who have their cameras turned on. If no one is sharing their video, then the Large gallery option will not be selectable in the menu.

FIGURE 3.36
Large gallery view showing 49 videos streams

Together Mode

Together mode lets you feel like you're in the same shared space with everyone during the meeting (see Figure 3.37). When there are at least five people in the meeting sharing their video, Together mode becomes available for you to choose. With Together mode, everyone's video appears in the same virtual space, which you can change to an assortment of scenes if you're a meeting organizer.

FIGURE 3.37
Together mode example

Focus

Focus mode is available when content is being shared. Use this view when you'd like to pay close attention to the content without the distraction of seeing people's video feeds.

PIN SOMEONE'S VIDEO

There are times you may want to pin someone's video to your view regardless of who is talking. To pin someone's video during a call, select More Options in their video feed (next to their name) and choose Pin.

REFRAME A VIDEO

Teams crops some videos to make them fit your screen better. If you want a different view of a particular video—for example, if someone is cropped out of the video or it only shows part of their face—select the More Options button in their video feed, and then choose Fit To Frame (see Figure 3.38) to see the entire video. Select Fill Frame (see Figure 3.39) to see a closer, cropped view.

FIGURE 3.38
Fit To Frame option of an attendee's video frame

FIGURE 3.39
Fill Frame option of an attendee's video frame

Recording a Meeting

If not disabled by the tenant administrator, users can record their Teams meetings and group calls to capture audio, video, and screen sharing activity. The recording happens in the cloud and is saved to OneDrive for Business or SharePoint Online. When a meeting is recorded, it's automatically permissioned to the people invited to the meeting and a link to the recording gets posted in the chat for the meeting. Meeting recordings for Teams will not capture shared notes, annotations, whiteboards, and embedded videos or animations embedded in a PowerPoint Live presentation. Anyone who meets the following criteria can start or stop a recording even if the meeting organizer is not present:

♦ Has Office 365 Enterprise E1, E3, E5, F3, A1, A2, A3, A5, M365 Business, Business Premium, or a Business Essentials license.

♦ Has recording enabled by IT admin.

♦ Is not a guest or not from another organization.

Recording will continue if the person who started the recording has left the meeting, and any participant who meets the criteria can manually stop recording any time. The recording will also automatically stop once everyone leaves the meeting, and if someone forgets to leave, the recording will automatically end after four hours. To record a meeting, you select the option in the meeting controls (see Figure 3.40).

FIGURE 3.40
Start recording a Teams meeting menu option

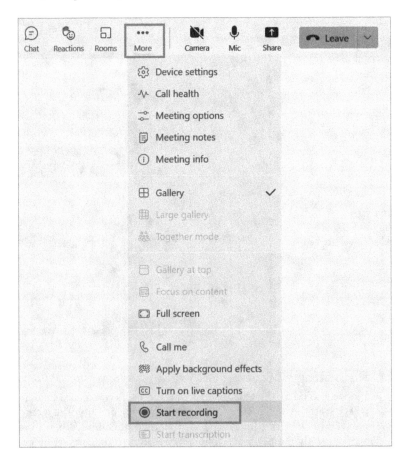

NOTE   You cannot do multiple recordings of the same meeting at the same time. If one person starts recording a meeting, the recording will be stored in the cloud and be made available to all participants. This includes participants who were invited to the meeting but didn't attend. Please visit `https://support.microsoft.com/en-us/office/ record-a-meeting-in-teams-34dfbe7f-b07d-4a27-b4c6-de62f1348c24#bkmk_find_ recordings`.

PRIVACY AND COMPLIANCE

When a meeting is being recorded in Teams, a notification to all participants will show up when the meeting recording starts. While Teams allows you to record all meetings, it is important to know the rules before recording as there are some places where you must legally get everyone's permission before you can record them. If any of the participants has a policy for compliance recording, the meeting will record according to the policy even if the participant is from another organization.

NOTE   For more information on the Microsoft Privacy Statement, please visit `http://aka.ms/ teamsprivacy`.

Meeting Notes

Video collaboration services are here to stay, and apps like Teams have been at the forefront offering remote conferencing solutions that some users depend on for their everyday work. While video calls are the primary aspect of conferencing services, there are other aspects that contribute to making your work more convenient and easier. We all have different ways of working, and I used OneNote to capture meeting notes until recently. Microsoft Teams has a native meeting note option that lets you capture notes for a meeting before, during, and after the meeting. The meeting notes created in a Teams meeting will be visible and accessible to other members of the meeting. To create a meeting note, simply open the meeting chat conversation and click Meeting Notes. You will see a Take Notes button, which you can click to initiate start taking notes (see Figure 3.41).

FIGURE 3.41
Take Notes button on the Meetings Notes tab

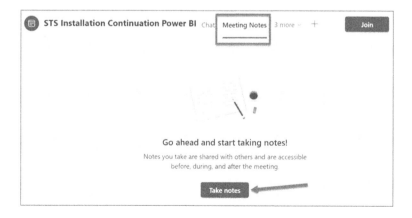

NOTE   To learn how to use automatic note taking in Microsoft Teams with meeting transcription, please visit `https://techcommunity.microsoft.com/t5/microsoft-mechanics-blog/automate-note-taking-in-microsoft-teams-with-meeting/ba-p/2242782`.

NOTE   Meeting participants have the option of viewing the transcription during the meeting if transcription is enabled. For more details on viewing live transcriptions, please visit `https://support.microsoft.com/en-us/office/view-live-transcription-in-a-teams-meeting-dc1a8f23-2e20-4684-885e-2152e06a4a8b`.

Meeting Etiquette and Tips

Since virtual meetings have become one of the primary means of communication, it is important to understand best practices and etiquette for Teams meetings as well as practices you should avoid. First let's talk about knowing when to mute and unmute your microphone during a virtual meeting. To help avoid a chaotic start, it is recommended to join a meeting muted as an attendee and then unmute when appropriate. It is also recommended to stay muted while you're not speaking. Failing to mute your microphone when you aren't speaking can be a major distraction because any noise you make or noise from your surroundings can be heard by everyone on the call. While noise cancelling headsets and noise canceling in Teams helps, it is still recommended to mute when not speaking. Also, don't forget to unmute when you are speaking. A common phrase heard these days when someone is trying to speak on mute is "You're on mute" so the best course of action is to stay alert and be ready to promptly flip your microphone on when it's your turn to talk.

Another recommendation for Teams meetings is to turn your camera on when possible. While the purpose of hosting a meeting may vary, it is more impactful when you can meet face-to-face. Turning your camera on for meetings is the next best thing to meeting in person. There may be instances where keeping your camera turned off is best, and it's important to use your judgement and only turn your camera on if you feel comfortable and prepared. One thing to consider when turning your camera on is determining if you should use a virtual background or background blur. Whether you're working from home, office, coffee shop or another location, blurring your background allows you to create a sense of professionalism and helps eliminate background distractions. Having a busy background could act as a major distraction for your teammates or the meeting host especially if you're not in a private location.

A few other tips is to follow a detailed agenda which helps boost meeting productivity. Do not over invite people and be mindful of time. If more time is needed, it is recommended to schedule a follow up call instead of keeping everyone over, and if you are going to run over ask participants if it is okay. Be mindful of personal or confidential information while sharing your screen. Don't interrupt other attendees. Only chime in after everyone has finished speaking or someone has called on you. You can also send a quick message in the chat feature if you want to add something during the call without verbally interrupting. Another important tip is to avoid getting distracted or showing boredom through body language during a call when your camera is turned on. If you need to do something while being on the call, turn your camera off and then turn it back on when appropriate.

Calls in Teams

Calls are at the core of what you can do in Teams. With many calling options and useful features at your disposal, you can communicate with people or groups in familiar ways.

Turn a Chat into a Call

You can easily turn a chat into a call with one simple click without having to host a Teams meeting. When you're in a chat you can select the Video or Audio call button to start a call with the person you are chatting with (see Figure 3.42). When you call another person, you'll see their profile picture on your screen (see Figure 3.43), and likewise when another person calls you (see Figure 3.44). These calls are private and won't appear in any team conversation; however, the entries for the calls will appear in your chat.

FIGURE 3.42
Video call and Audio call buttons

FIGURE 3.43
Calling another person dialog box

FIGURE 3.44
Person being called
dialog box

Adding Additional People to Call Started from Chat

There may be a situation in which you are on a call with a colleague and you determine you need to loop another person into the call. Instead of creating a meeting, you can add more people to your call by going to the People panel (see Figure 3.45) and searching for the person you want to add to the current call (see Figure 3.46). As soon as you invite someone to join the Teams call, you will see the person get added with a status of Calling (see Figure 3.47) and the person you are calling will see they are getting an incoming call from a group chat (see Figure 3.48).

FIGURE 3.45
Invite Someone Or Dial
A Number option to add
people to a call

FIGURE 3.46
Adding another
person to a call

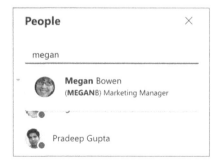

FIGURE 3.47
Calling notification in
People panel

FIGURE 3.48
Group chat call
dialog box

See Your Call History

Call history is available any time so you can review your list of past calls (including missed calls) and easily call those people back. To access your call history, go to Calls and then click History (see Figure 3.49).

FIGURE 3.49
Call history example

Recommendations and Tips

One of the questions asked when providing Teams training was "Are there any recommendations on how we should be naming our meetings?" While each organization can be different, some companies have adopted naming standards. For example, at Core BTS, they do Rough Order of Magnitude reviews internally and present the ROM to the customer. For an internal call, the meeting would be named "Internal - Client Name ROM Review." The meeting with the client would be named "Core BTS/Client Name ROM Review." This is helpful to be able to easily see on the calendar which calls are internal and which are with customers. It also helps to navigate in Teams when you want to go back and access the chat, meeting notes, or whiteboard that was used during the calls.

Live Events

Microsoft Teams live events are an extension of Teams meetings that can be used to schedule and produce events that stream live video and content to large online audiences. Live events are considered the next version of Skype Meeting Broadcast. Live events are intended for one-to-many communications where the host of the event is leading the interactions, and the audience participation is primarily to view the content shared by the host. Instead of using the chat feature like you would in a Teams meeting, the participants interact through a moderated Q&A. Anyone can attend a live event, including users without a license.

NOTE   For best practices on producing Live events, please visit `https://support.microsoft.com/en-us/office/best-practices-for-producing-a-teams-live-event-e500370e-4dd1-4187-8b48-af10ef02cf42`.

Event Group Roles

Large live streaming events typically have several people working behind the scenes to make the event successful:

◆ **Organizer**: Schedules a live event and ensures the event is set up with the right permissions for attendees and the event group, who will manage the event.

◆ **Producer**: As a host, makes sure attendees have a great viewing experience by controlling the live event stream.

◆ **Presenter**: Presents audio, video, or a screen to the live event, or moderates Q&A (see Figure 3.50).

◆ **Attendee**: A viewer. Watches the event live or on-demand, using DVR controls, either anonymously or authenticated. Attendees can participate in Q&A during the webinar (see Figure 3.51).

FIGURE 3.50
Live Event presenter
view

FIGURE 3.51
Live Event attendee view
showing Q&A

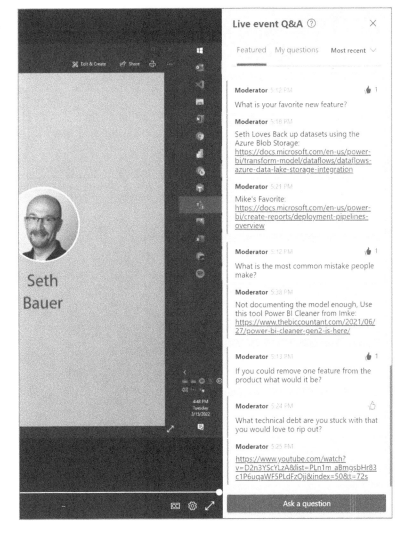

The interface will look different and have features enabled and disabled based on role. For example, when an external presenter joins they will be muted and the control will be disabled for the presenter. Before the presenter can present, the producer must promote them, which then enables the controls to unmute and share their screen. The producers will have controls that the presenters will not be able to see. Chat is available only for the organizers, producers, and presenters, which can be used to communicate as a back channel that attendees do not see during the broadcast.

Live Event Permissions

When you create a live event you will need to choose the live event permissions, which are People And Groups, Org-Wide, or Public. The Public permission will only be available if your Teams IT admin has enabled the permission at the tenant level. If it hasn't been enabled, then the Public option will be grayed out (see Figure 3.52). If your IT admin has enabled the permission level to everyone, then you will have the ability to choose Public (see Figure 3.53).

FIGURE 3.52
Public live event choice grayed out

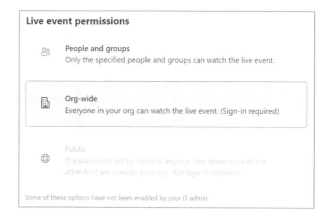

FIGURE 3.53
Public live event choice selected

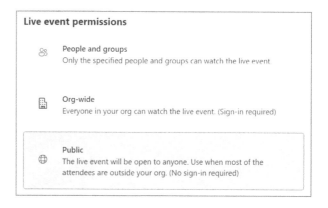

People And Groups

The People And Groups live event permission option will allow you to add people or groups to the live event (see Figure 3.54).

Figure 3.54
People And Groups live
event permission option

Live event permissions

Give permission to:

	People and groups	Add a person or a group
	Only the specified people and groups can watch the live event.	

Patti Fernandez
PattiF@M365x19076970.OnMicrosoft...   ×

	Org-wide	
	Everyone in your org can watch the live event. (Sign-in required)	

Allan Deyoung
AllanD@M365x19076970.OnMicroso...   ×

	Public	
	The live event will be open to anyone. Use when most of the attendees are outside your org. (No sign-in required)	

Debra Berger
DebraB@M365x19076970.OnMicros...   ×

Live Events Production Options

After you decide what type of live event you want to schedule (People And Groups, Org-Wide, or Public) you then set the options for how you will produce your live event (see Figure 3.55).

Figure 3.55
Live event
production options

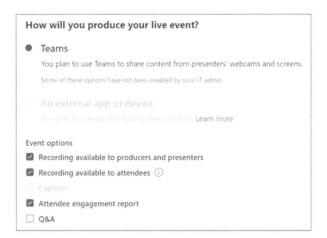

How will you produce your live event?

● **Teams**

You plan to use Teams to share content from presenters' webcams and screens.

Some of these options have not been enabled by your IT admin

○ An external app or device

You plan to use another tool to share content. Learn more

Event options

☑ Recording available to producers and presenters
☑ Recording available to attendees ⓘ
☐ Captions
☑ Attendee engagement report
☐ Q&A

Scheduling

Teams enables the organizers to create an event with the appropriate attendee permissions, designate event team members, select a production method, and invite attendees (see Figure 3.56).

Production

The video input is the foundation of the live event and can vary from a single webcam to a multi-camera professional video production setup. Live events in Microsoft 365 support streaming an event produced in Teams using a webcam or produced using an external app or device. You can choose these options depending on the production's team project requirements and budget.

FIGURE 3.56
Scheduling a new
live event

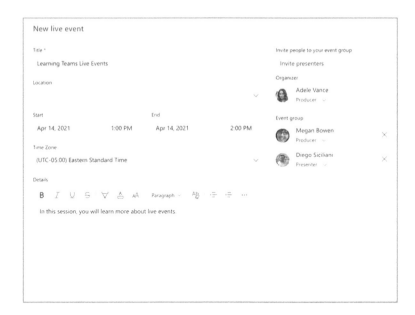

There are two ways to produce Teams live events:

◆ **Teams**: This production method allows users to produce their live events in Teams using
their webcam or using A/V input from Teams room systems. This option is the best and
quickest option if you want to use the audio and video devices connected to the PC or are
inviting remote presenters to participate in the event. This option allows users to easily
use their webcams and share their screen as input in the event.

◆ **External app or device**: External encoders allow users to produce their live events directly
from an external hardware or software-based encoder with Stream. This option is best if
you already have studio-quality equipment (for example, media mixers) that support
streaming to a Real-time Messaging Protocol (RTMP) service. This type of production is
typically used in large-scale events such as executive town halls, where a single stream
from a media mixer is broadcasted to the audience.

Streaming Platform

The live event streaming platform is made up of the following pieces:

◆ **Azure Media Services**: Azure Media Services gives you broadcast-quality video streaming services to reach larger audiences on today's most popular mobile devices. Media
Services enhances accessibility, distribution, and scalability, and makes it easy and
cost-effective to stream content to your local or worldwide audiences—all while protecting your content.

◆ **Azure Content Delivery Network (CDN)**: Once your stream goes live, it's delivered
through the Azure Content Delivery Network (CDN). Azure Media Services provides
integrated CDN for streaming endpoints. This allows the streams to be viewed worldwide
with no buffering.

Enterprise Content Delivery Network

Enterprise Content Delivery Network (eCDN) is used to take video content from the internet and distribute it throughout the entire enterprise without impacting network performance. The current certified eCDN partners you can use to optimize your network for live events include:

◆ Hive

◆ Kollective

◆ Ramp

◆ Riverbend

Attendee Experience

The attendee experience is the most important aspect of live events. To have a smooth experience for your attendees it's critical they can participate in the live event without having issues.

The attendee experience uses the following:

◆ **Stream Player**: For events produced in Teams.

◆ **Azure Media Player**: For events produced in an external app or device.

Both the Stream Player and the Azure Media Player work across desktops, browsers, and mobile devices. Microsoft 365 and Office 365 provide both Yammer and Teams as the two collaboration hubs, and the live attendee experience is integrated into both collaboration tools.

Live Event Usage Report

Real-time usage analytics for live events are available to tenant admins through the Microsoft Teams admin center. This report includes the activity overview of the live events held within the organization, and the admin can view the event usage information, including event status, start time, views, and production type.

Webinars

Webinar is not a new term as many products have provided webinar capabilities for many years. GoToMeeting and WebEx have common webinar platforms many organizations use. Webinars are different than meetings in that they are meant to be more controlled. They are dynamic and could be a presentation, lecture, workshop, or another type of hosted online event where the audience remotely attends. You can easily schedule a webinar by selecting Webinar from the + New Meeting drop-down menu in the Teams calendar (see Figure 3.57).

FIGURE 3.57
Webinar option shown
in New Meeting
drop-down in Teams

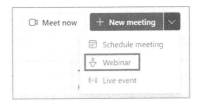

When you create a new webinar (see Figure 3.58) you will need to provide a title, required presenters, date and time, and any other optional or required fields. You can also change the response options (see Figure 3.59) and registration requirement (see Figure 3.60).

FIGURE 3.58
New webinar being created in Teams

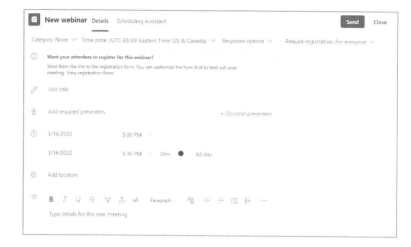

FIGURE 3.59
Webinar Response Options drop-down menu

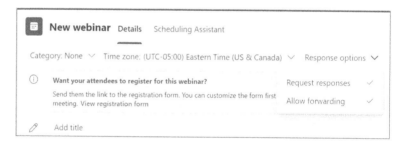

FIGURE 3.60
Webinar registration requirement drop-down menu options

Breakout Rooms

Breakout rooms are a feature available for meeting organizers that allow you to divide attendees into separate groups during an online meeting. You can only create breakout rooms using the Microsoft Teams desktop client (Windows or Mac) and you cannot use them with meetings that have more than 300 attendees. Some common scenarios to use breakout rooms include educators needing to divide students into groups or for meetings that require breaking out participants into groups.

NOTE   For more details on breakout rooms, please visit https://support.microsoft.com/
   en-us/office/use-breakout-rooms-in-teams-meetings-7de1f48a-da07-466c-a5ab-
   4ebace28e461.

Audio Conferencing

Audio Conferencing in Microsoft 365 and Office 365 enables users to dial in to meetings from their phones. Audio Conferencing allows up to 250 phone attendees in a meeting.

What Is Audio Conferencing?

Allowing users to call in (dial in) to meetings is useful for those who are on the road and can't attend the meeting through Microsoft Teams. Some other scenarios where Audio Conferencing can be beneficial include when:

◆   Internet connectivity is limited, or bandwidth is too low and causing issues with call quality.

◆   A meeting is audio only.

◆   An attendee tried to join a Teams meeting but failed.

To use Audio Conferencing, you only need to set it up for the people who plan to schedule or lead meetings. Meeting attendees dialing in don't need any licenses assigned to them as it's only required for the organizers.

Conferencing Bridges and Phone Numbers

Conferencing bridges enable people to dial into meetings using a phone. You can use the default settings for a conference bridge or change the phone numbers to use a toll or toll-free number, as well as other settings such as setting a PIN and default language.

NOTE   For more details on Audio Conferencing licensing, please visit https://aka.ms/
   TeamsArchSolutionsPosters and https://aka.ms/CloudArchModels.

The Bottom Line

Meetings in Teams.   Teams makes it easy to collaborate with people inside and outside of your organization with the ability to meet with people using audio, video, and screen sharing. You can also easily add additional devices or transfer a device to a meeting you have joined.

Master It   You joined a meeting from your phone but during the meeting realized you need to present something from your computer. How can you transfer the meeting from your phone to your computer to share your screen in the meeting without having to hang up and rejoin?

Calls in Teams. You can start a call from a chat any time in Teams regardless if you are using the app or a browser. There are times when you may start a chat with a colleague and then decide to continue the conversation through a Teams call. This feature is great because it does not require you to schedule a meeting.

Master It You are chatting with your colleague on an issue you are having, and your colleague decides to call you directly from the chat to discuss more. During this call you both decide you need to loop in another colleague to help provide feedback as well. How do you add another person to your active call?

Live Events. Teams provides the ability to schedule live events. Live events are great to use when you need to have more than 250 attendees. When you create a live event it will default to the People And Groups permission level; however, you can change it to be Org-Wide or Public.

Master It You need to create a public live event but the option to choose Public for the live event permission is grayed out. How do you enable your tenant to allow public live events so this option will become available?

Audio Conferencing. Teams provides an option where you can create meetings to include a dial-in number so attendees can call in when joining a meeting. This option is not available by default as it is dependent on an audio conferencing add-on license and configuration.

Master It You have people both inside and outside of your organization that you meet on a regular basis. Some of the people are on the road and have issues joining through Teams. How do you make it easier for those who are on the road to call in without having to join from the Teams app or browser?

Chapter 4

Extending Teams with Apps

With the change to hybrid and remote work, leaders in organizations are looking for ways to improve their employees' collaboration experience. Most organizations have moved to Microsoft Teams or other online platforms for collaboration to support this new way of working. Microsoft Teams is a great collaboration tool, but how can organizations improve their user experience? How can they streamline business processes external to Microsoft Teams and make it easier for users to access what they need? The answer to that is by extending Microsoft Teams with apps.

You can install Microsoft apps, third-party apps, and custom apps. Microsoft Teams is an extensible platform where you can build your own custom apps that can be as simple or as complex as you need. You can build apps for an individual, team, entire organization, or for all Teams users.

IN THIS CHAPTER, YOU WILL LEARN THE FOLLOWING

- ◆ Understanding the Teams app platform and apps in Teams
- ◆ Core workloads and extensibility options
- ◆ Benefits of using apps in Teams
- ◆ App templates and integrations
- ◆ Extending Teams with the Power Platform

Teams App Platform

This section provides an overview of the Microsoft Teams app platform to understand core workloads and the types of apps that can be developed and deployed in your Teams tenant.

Core Workloads and Extensible Platform

The core workloads in Teams enables communication through chats, meetings, and calls as well as collaboration with deeply integrated Microsoft 365 apps. Teams can go a step further by connecting all your systems and processes to help get more work done (see Figure 4.1).

FIGURE 4.1
Extensible platform
diagram

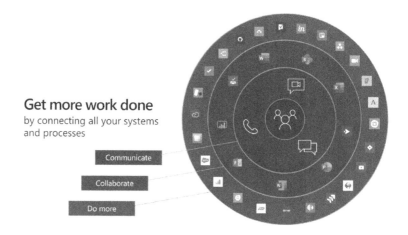

Get more work done
by connecting all your systems
and processes

Communicate

Collaborate

Do more

Types of Apps in Microsoft Teams

There are three buckets of apps for Teams (see Figure 4.2): Microsoft apps, third-party apps, and custom apps.

MICROSOFT APPS

Microsoft apps are apps specifically published by Microsoft. Teams integrates with many applications in the Microsoft 365 suite such as OneDrive, Excel, Word, SharePoint Online, OneNote, and more.

THIRD-PARTY APPS

For added productivity, Teams integrates with apps outside of the Microsoft domain such as ADP, Salesforce, ServiceNow, GitHub, and more. In the Teams app store, you can choose from over 1,000 popular apps to make your work easier every day. The cost per app varies from free to subscription-based, and you may be able to leverage enterprise licenses you already have. For example, if you are already licensed and using ServiceNow, you can use the ServiceNow Teams app at no extra cost. Third-party apps can be trusted, as they go through an approval attestation process with Microsoft before they are published to the app store for Teams.

CUSTOM APPS

You can quickly build low-code custom apps for Teams with little or no development experience, or develop more advanced custom app solutions to meet your business needs using the Teams extensible platform. Custom apps provide unlimited possibilities with low-code solutions through the Power Platform, predefined app templates, or you can build apps from scratch.

NOTE To learn more about building your own custom apps, please visit `https://docs`
`.microsoft.com/en-us/microsoftteams/platform/overview`.

FIGURE 4.2
Microsoft Apps,
Third-party Apps, and
Custom Apps

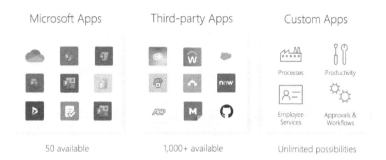

Understanding Apps in Teams

Teams apps are a combination of capabilities built on the Microsoft Teams Platform extending the Teams client (web, mobile, and desktop) with web services you host. Teams app capabilities can range from simple to complex.

Teams App Capabilities

A Teams app can have one or all of the following capabilities:

◆ Bots

◆ Tabs

◆ Personal Apps

◆ Messaging Extensions

◆ Meeting Extensions

◆ Webhooks and Connectors

You can install already made apps available in the Teams apps store (see Figure 4.3) or you can develop and install your own custom Teams app. When you click an app in the Teams apps store, a dialog will appear with information about the app, including the app title, description, publisher information, list of capabilities, and permissions required for the app (see Figure 4.4). You can select the drop-down Add button to choose where you want to install the app. The options available in the drop-down will depend on the capabilities the app supports.

TABS

Tabs are embedded web pages in Teams that can be added as part of a channel inside a team (see Figure 4.5), group chat, or inside a personal app scoped for a single user. You can add a new tab to a team at any time by clicking the + icon next to the tabs. From the dialog (see Figure 4.6), you will see a list of all available apps with the tab capability that you can choose from.

FIGURE 4.3
Teams app store

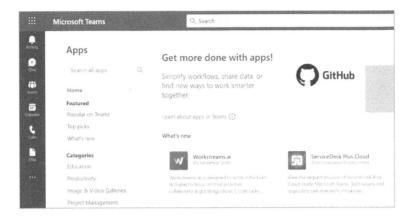

FIGURE 4.4
SurveyMonkey app
information highlighting
capabilities and
permissions

FIGURE 4.5
Teams tabs

Tabs are great for embedding files such as Word, PDF, and PowerPoint, or for embedding a SharePoint site's home page. When you select an app to add as a tab, a dialog will appear with options. The options available will vary depending on the type of app you are adding as a tab. For example, if you want to embed a PowerPoint file you will have a dialog that allows you to set the tab name as well as set the PowerPoint file you want to embed in the tab (see Figure 4.7). After you click Save, the PowerPoint file will be embedded as a new tab within your team (see Figure 4.8). Once a tab is added to a channel you can rename, delete, or reorder the positioning of the tab.

FIGURE 4.6
Dialog of tab apps

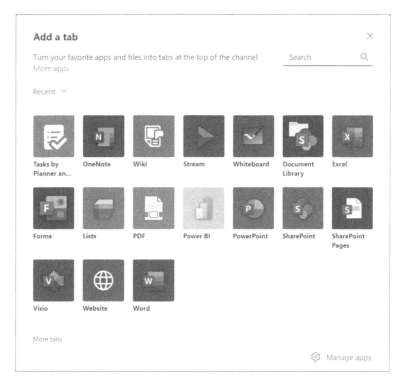

FIGURE 4.7
Adding a PowerPoint file as a tab in Teams

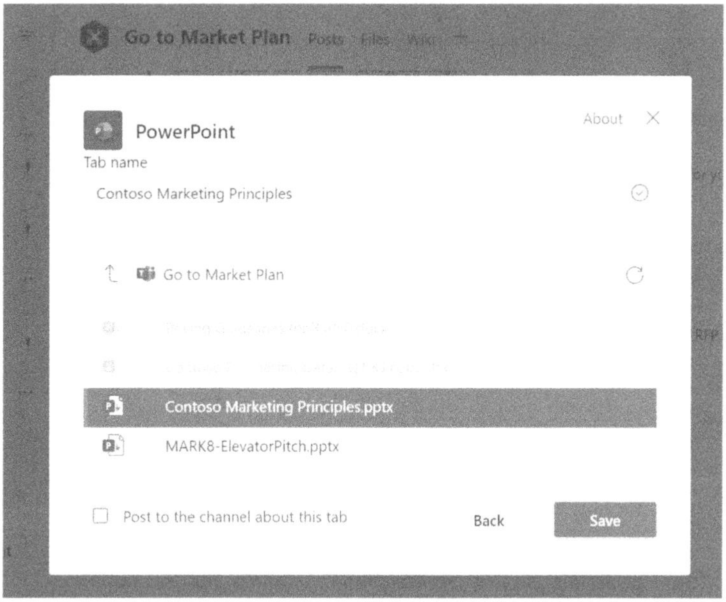

FIGURE 4.8
PowerPoint file
displayed in Teams as an
embedded tab

BOTS

A bot (otherwise known as a chatbot or conversational bot) is an app that users can interact with in a conversational way using text, graphics, or speech. A bot interaction can be a simple question and answer or can be a complex conversation providing access to services. Conversational bots allow users to interact with a web service through text, interactive cards, and through task modules. Bots can be used in Teams through channel and group chat conversations or through one-on-one conversations. A bot behaves differently depending on the conversation with the end user of where the bot runs in:

- **Bots in channel and group chat conversation:** To invoke, the user is required to @mention the bot in the channel or group chat (see Figure 4.9). After the @mention you can type a command or select a choice if presented with suggestions (see Figure 4.10).

- **Bots in a one-to-one conversation:** Invoking does not require the user to @mention. All messages sent by the user routes to the bot. For example, to create a new poll using Microsoft Forms you can simply type @form and then click + Create A New Poll (see Figure 4.11). To start a conversation with the ServiceNow for Teams bot all the user needs to do is type a message such as "Hi" to start the conversation (see Figure 4.12).

In the Forms bot example, if you click + Create A New Poll a dialog will appear to create a new Forms poll (see Figure 4.11).

FIGURE 4.9
Using @mention to
invoke Forms bot in
channel chat
conversation

FIGURE 4.10
Forms bot showing
suggested choices

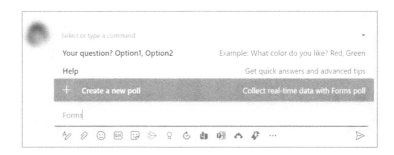

FIGURE 4.11
Create a new poll with
sample question

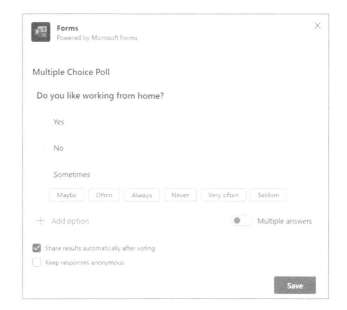

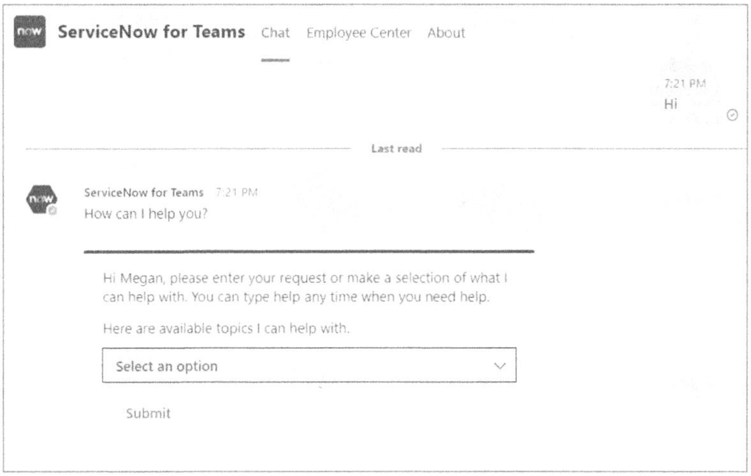

FIGURE 4.12
ServiceNow for Teams
bot conversation

MESSAGING EXTENSIONS

Messaging extensions enable users to interact with a web service that is invoked through the compose box in Teams. Messaging extensions use the Bot framework messaging schema and secure communication protocol. Whether you are composing a new message or replying to one, the compose box will have a list of icons on desktop clients (see Figure 4.13) and mobile clients (see Figure 4.14). Messaging extensions are also available through the channel posts. To access, simply hover over the upper-right side of a message and click the . . . (see Figure 4.15). Click More Actions to display additional available messaging extensions (see Figure 4.16).

FIGURE 4.13
Desktop example:
Compose box highlighting messaging extensions icons

FIGURE 4.14
Mobile example:
Compose box highlighting messaging extensions icons

FIGURE 4.15
Channel message showing available messaging extensions

FIGURE 4.16
More Actions link to
display additional
messaging extensions
for channel post

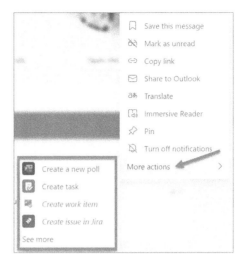

There are two types of messaging extensions commands: *action commands* and *search commands*. Action commands are triggered from the compose message area, command box, or from a message. They are used to present users with a modal pop-up to collect or display information. Search commands allow users to query a service and post the information in the form of a card.

Meeting Extensions

Teams meetings now have the capability to add apps to enhance the user experience to make your meetings more productive and engaging. Meetings apps can be used for each stage of the meeting life cycle. The meeting life cycle has three stages:

◆ Pre-meeting

◆ In-meeting

◆ Post-meeting

You can integrate bots, messaging extensions, and tabs in each stage of the meeting life cycle. There are currently around 65 apps for Teams meetings available in the Teams app store. To see a list of available meetings apps, click Meetings under the App Features filter (see Figure 4.17). For example, if you want to add the Forms app to a meeting you would need to select Add To A Meeting (see Figure 4.18).

Webhooks and Connectors

Webhooks and connectors provide a way for you to connect web services to channels in Teams. It's a simple way to push and send data outside of the Teams client. Incoming webhooks allow you to post messages from apps to Teams. Outgoing webhooks can send messages to web services with @mention. The creation of an incoming webhook starts with adding the Incoming Webhook app in the Teams apps store (see Figure 4.19).

FIGURE 4.17
Filtering apps with the
meetings capability in
the Teams apps store

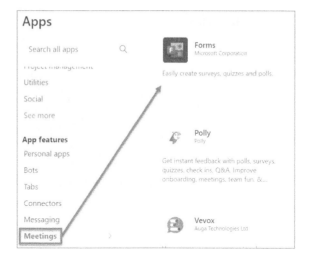

FIGURE 4.18
Forms app highlighting
Meeting capability and
Add To A Meeting
menu option

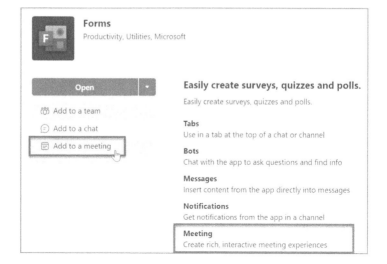

FIGURE 4.19
Incoming webhook
connector in Teams
apps store

NOTE   To learn more about webhooks and connectors, please visit `https://docs.microsoft.com/en-us/power-virtual-agents/teams/fundamentals-what-is-power-virtual-agents-teams`.

Apps Scope

The apps scope is an area where a user can use a Teams app. Apps can have one or more scopes, which includes channels, chats, meetings, and personal.

Personal Apps

An app with the personal app capability is an app targeted for interactions with a single user. It provides a personal view that is unique to each individual user. Personal apps are available to install from the Teams apps store (see Figure 4.20) or can also be installed for all users at the tenant level.

FIGURE 4.20
Personal Apps link in the Teams apps store

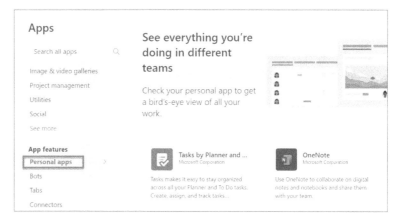

Microsoft Apps

Microsoft apps built and published for Teams available through the apps store will show Microsoft Corporation as the publisher under the app name (see Figure 4.21).

FIGURE 4.21
Examples Microsoft apps available in the Teams apps store

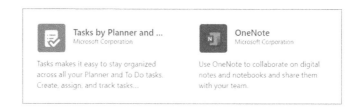

Third-Party Apps

There are many benefits to allowing and using third-party apps in Teams. This is especially beneficial if you're already using services outside of Microsoft such as Smartsheet, ServiceNow, ADP, and more.

MYTHS OF USING THIRD-PARTY APPS IN TEAMS

Many organizations disable allowing third-party apps in Teams because of security concerns or lack of understanding what apps can and cannot access in Teams. Here are the top four myths of using apps in Teams:

◆ **Allowing third-party apps will create licensing headaches.** Many of the apps in Teams are free or leverage existing enterprise licenses.

◆ **Apps will access all my confidential files and conversations.** Apps can only access files you explicitly send to that app service, and they can only read messages when the app is explicitly mentioned in a message.

◆ **Apps will access all my personal information and send spam.** App developers can only access basic personal information. Sending spam violates Microsoft's app store policies and will result in the app getting taken down.

◆ **It is inconvenient and messy to uninstall an app after setting it up.** Users can uninstall an app personally with two clicks, and admins can uninstall an app tenant-wide with two clicks.

THIRD-PARTY APPS USE CASE

The types of business solution opportunities around teamwork are quite endless from industries like airline, retail, healthcare, legal firm, real estate, different industries, and different functions. (see Figure 4.22). If you deliver consulting services, you can envision with your customers, understand their business process and teamwork needs, and connect Teams to the tools and services they use every day to help them fully realize the value of Teams.

FIGURE 4.22
Industry vertical and
horizontal solution
needs examples

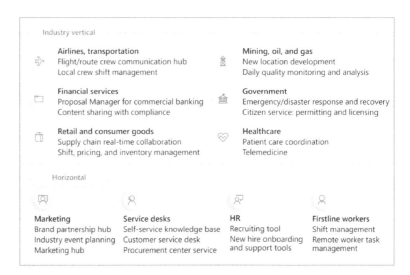

If your organization fits in one of these example industries or another with different required functions, you can leverage many third-party apps to fit your business scenarios. You can identify third-party apps in the Teams apps store that do not have Microsoft Corporation under the app name. Some common third-party apps many organizations use are Jira Cloud, Polly, monday.com, and Zoho Projects (see Figure 4.23).

FIGURE 4.23
Example third-party apps in the Teams apps store

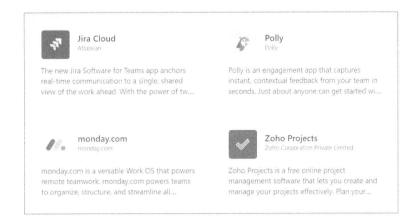

EXAMPLE USE CASE: DIAGNOSIS/REMEDIATION COMMON INCIDENTS

A large amount of IT's time is spent reacting to and solving problems. Many of the common issues can be easily solved without IT engagement. How can IT resources be freed up to engage in more impactful projects? Can this be solved through apps in Teams? The answer to the last question is yes. Example third-party apps that fit the preceding use case are IT Support and Help Desk apps such as ServiceNow, Jira, and Zendesk (see Figure 4.24). For this use case, we will use ServiceNow.

FIGURE 4.24
IT Support and Help Desk third-party apps

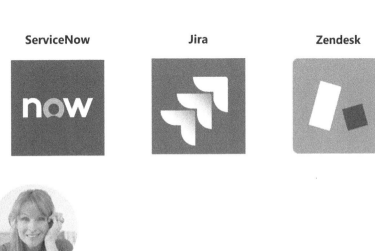

Megan Bowen, End User

Megan is having issues where her mail client is acting slow. She can access websites and other applications are working. Her internet connection seems fine, but she doesn't know why her mail client is slow. Megan opens the Now Virtual Agent chat in Teams and begins a conversation with the bot. The Now bot welcomes Megan and provides her with a drop-down list of options to choose from (see Figure 4.25).

FIGURE 4.25
Megan begins a conversation with the Now bot for help

Megan is presented with a list of options to choose from in a drop-down menu. She chooses Email Issues and then clicks Submit (see Figure 4.26). The bot responds with a list of choices based on Email Issues. Megan chooses Mail Client Is Slow and waits for the bot to respond. The bot responds with some solutions to try and asks if the steps worked for her (see Figure 4.27). Megan proceeds with closing her mail client and re-opening it. By doing that, the issue is resolved, so she goes back to the bot conversation and responds with Yes. Since Megan responded with a Yes that the steps worked for her, the bot ends the conversation (see Figure 4.28).

FIGURE 4.26
Megan chooses and submits her option

FIGURE 4.27
Bot presents Megan
with solutions to try

FIGURE 4.28
Bot ends conversation
since Megan
responded with Yes

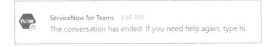

Extending with Custom Apps

If you have a business need that cannot be addressed with a Microsoft app or a third-party app in Teams, another option you have is to build your own custom apps for Teams. There are many different types of custom apps for Teams you can build and install into your Teams tenant (see Figure 4.29). You can build Power Platform solutions for Teams using Power BI, Power Apps, Power Automate, and Power Virtual Agents. Another option is to download and install predefined app templates Microsoft built and published to GitHub.

Teams App Templates

Microsoft Teams app templates are community-driven, prebuilt Teams apps for common line-of-business scenarios. App templates are designed to help you transform your business scenario needs and engage with employees inside of Teams. There are currently over 50 app templates available through an online gallery, and it continues to grow. Benefits of app templates include:

◆ **Plug 'n' play experience:** Minimal configuration needed and no coding required.

◆ **One-Click Deployment:** Automated experience to deploy the app to your own instance of Azure within minutes. Bring the experience to Teams seamlessly.

◆ **Secure, configurable, and extensible:** Open sourced so you can own, brand, configure, and extend to your needs.

FIGURE 4.29
Custom Apps
possibilities

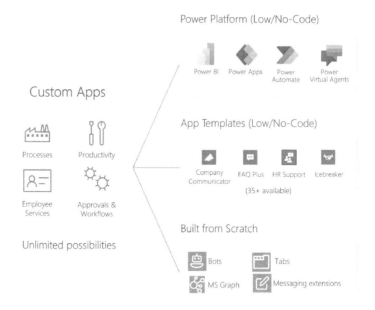

REQUEST A TEAM USE CASE

One of the most popular templates and use cases is the Request A Team app. The common ask has been giving users the ability to request having a team created through an approval and provisioning process. The Request A Team app template is the best solution for this use case that you can deploy to your tenant. This template optimizes new team creation for your enterprise organization. It also supports standardization and best practices when creating new team instances through integration of:

- Wizard-guided request form
- Embedded approval process
- Request status dashboard
- Automated team builds

The solution is a Power Platform solution and is available to download from GitHub. All instructions for the solution are provided online. You can install the solution as-is or modify it to fit your needs. The Request A Team app template consists of:

- **Power App**—App is surfaced in Teams with screens controlled based on permissions.
- **Flow**—Used for the Teams approval process. The flow sends an adaptive card to MS Teams and saves the response in the SharePoint list.
- **Logic App**—Used for the Team creation set to run at a scheduled interval. Will provision new teams that have been approved from the Flow.
- **SharePoint lists**—All data for the Power App is driven by SharePoint lists.

SharePoint Lists Used for Data

There are three SharePoint lists used for the app. The first, named Team Request Settings, is used for the configuration values needed for the Power App (see Figure 4.30). The second SharePoint list, named Teams Templates, contains all the templates users can use to create a team (see Figure 4.31). You can customize this list to only include the templates you want to allow. The third list, named Teams Requests, is used to store all the requests that come in from the Power App (see Figure 4.32).

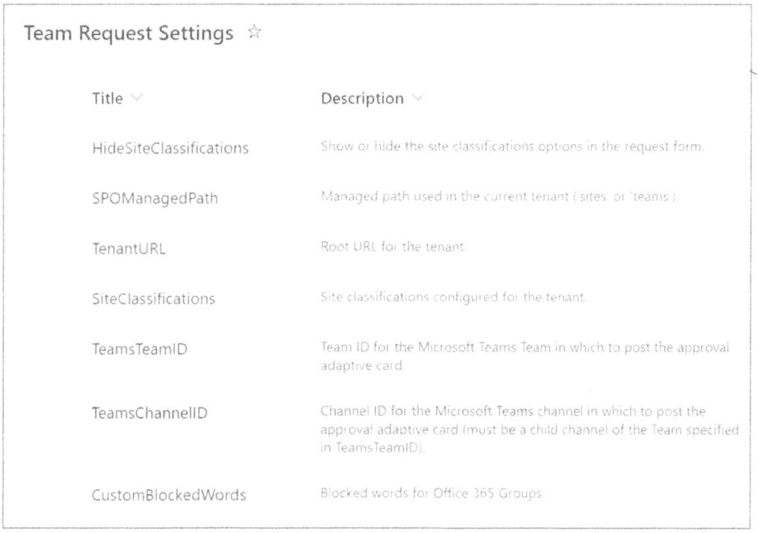

FIGURE 4.30
Team Request Settings
SharePoint list

Team Request Settings ☆

Title ⌄	Description ⌄
HideSiteClassifications	Show or hide the site classifications options in the request form.
SPOManagedPath	Managed path used in the current tenant (sites or teams).
TenantURL	Root URL for the tenant.
SiteClassifications	Site classifications configured for the tenant.
TeamsTeamID	Team ID for the Microsoft Teams Team in which to post the approval adaptive card.
TeamsChannelID	Channel ID for the Microsoft Teams channel in which to post the approval adaptive card (must be a child channel of the Team specified in TeamsTeamID).
CustomBlockedWords	Blocked words for Office 365 Groups.

FIGURE 4.31
Teams Templates
SharePoint list

Teams Templates ☆

Title ⌄	Description ⌄
Company-wide	Designed for internal communication and collaboration that are relevant for the entire company. You can use the General channel for company-wide announcements, industry news or executive posts.
Executives	Template for an executive team.
Departmental	Template for departmental teams.

FIGURE 4.32
Teams Requests
SharePoint list
displaying sam-
ple requests

App Surfaced by Users via Teams Tab

Once installed and configured, you can embed the Request A Team Power App directly into Teams as a tab (see Figure 4.33). Users can then access the app and request to have a team created from scratch or from a template. The user requesting a team will be guided through a wizard process. The options available through the wizard steps will vary depending on if they chose to Build New or Create From A Template. The user will be asked if they want the team to be Private or Public and then they will continue through the wizard process (see Figure 4.34).

FIGURE 4.33
Request a Team Power
App displayed in
Teams as a tab

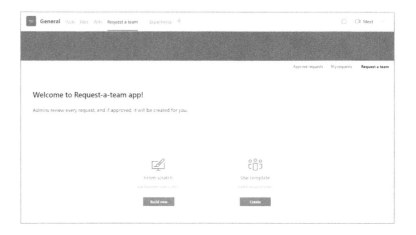

In this example, a new team request is being entered for building a new team from scratch. The user will put in the desired Team Name, Description, and Business Reason. They will not be able to click the Next button until they click Check Availability. When the users clicks the button, a flow is triggered to run that checks to see if the team name is already being used. The flow checks by seeing if a Microsoft 365 group and SharePoint site already exists. If the team name is not available, the user will see a status message in the app saying "Team name is taken. Try again" as shown in Figure 4.35. If it's available, the user will see a status message in the app saying "Team name is available" as shown in Figure 4.36. The next step after the team informa-tion is to choose two owners and optionally add members (see Figure 4.37).

FIGURE 4.34
Team information
screen example

FIGURE 4.35
Team name not
available message

FIGURE 4.36
Team name available
message with additional
information

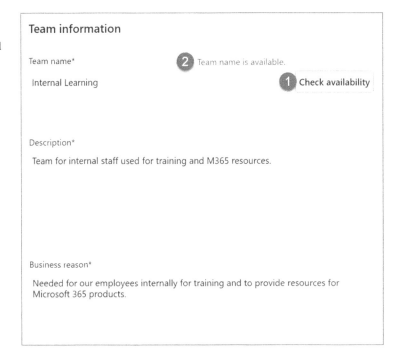

FIGURE 4.37
Add Members step
showing two owners
being added with
no members

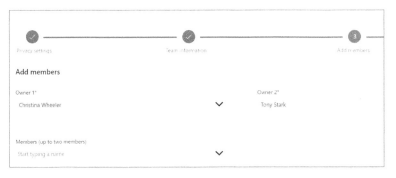

In the final step, the user will see a preview of the request to give them an option to review before submitting the request (see Figure 4.38). Once the user clicks the Submit button, a dialog will appear that states the request has been submitted as shown in Figure 4.39. After the submittal, the requester can check the status of their request (s) by clicking Check Status, which will take them to the My Requests section of the app (see Figure 4.40). Once a request is submitted, the request is written to a SharePoint list, which then triggers another flow for the team request approval process (see Figure 4.41).

FIGURE 4.38
Review And Submit last
step preview before user
clicks Submit

FIGURE 4.39
Request Submitted
dialog that displays after
user submits the request

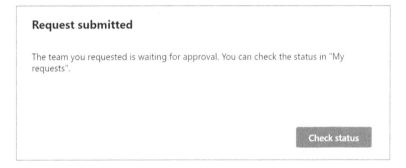

FIGURE 4.40
My Requests tab in app
showing example of
team requests submis-
sions for user

For the approval process, a secure team is set up during the installation process that only the approvers will be able to access. The approval flow will post an adaptive card to the Teams channel and then wait for a response for the approver to Approve or Reject the request (see Figure 4.42). The approver can approve or reject directly within the adaptive card and provide optional comments (see Figure 4.43).

Once the approver clicks the Submit button, the flow is triggered to continue to run the remaining steps. The actions it takes is dependent on whether the request was approved or rejected. In this example, the request was approved so the flow runs the steps under the If Yes branch (see Figure 4.44). The flow updates the adaptive card in Teams and updates the status of the request in the SharePoint list (see Figure 4.45 and Figure 4.46).

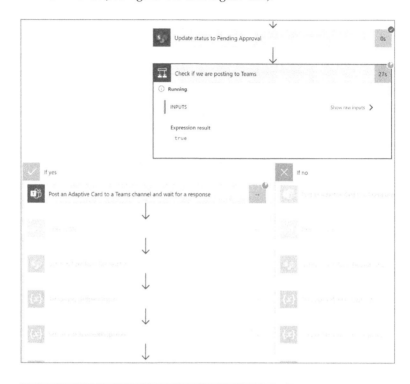

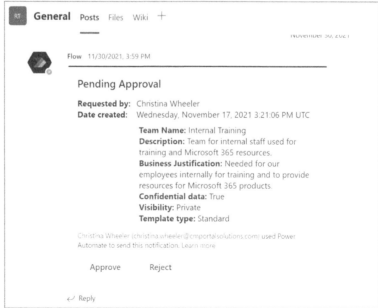

FIGURE 4.43
Pending Approval
example of approving
request in the
adaptive card

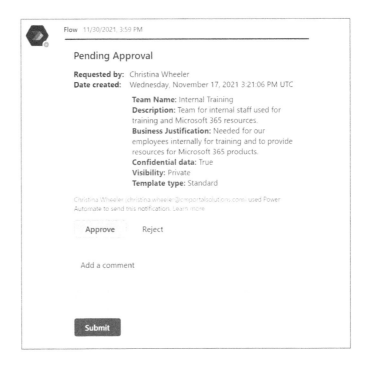

FIGURE 4.44
Flow triggered after
response from adaptive
card and continues
remaining steps

FIGURE 4.45
Approval flow showing
executed actions

FIGURE 4.46
Adaptive card and
SharePoint list status
updated example

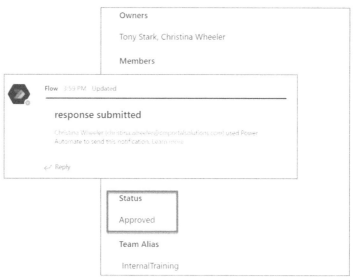

Teams Provisioning Azure Logic App

A Logic App in Microsoft Azure is used for the provisioning of the approved team requests. You
can change the configuration of the Logic App to run at your desired interval. In this example,
the scheduled time is set to run once a day (see Figure 4.47).

To test, you can manually trigger the Logic App or wait for it to run at the scheduled interval. When running, you can see the steps in real time (see Figure 4.48) the same as you can with a flow in Power Automate. The provisioning process takes around five minutes to complete for each team it is creating, and you can see the status in the Run history (see Figure 4.49). Once the team is created, the user who made the request will receive an email (see Figure 4.50) and the new team will also show up in Teams (see Figure 4.51).

FIGURE 4.47
Logic App in Microsoft Azure showing the frequency setting you can change

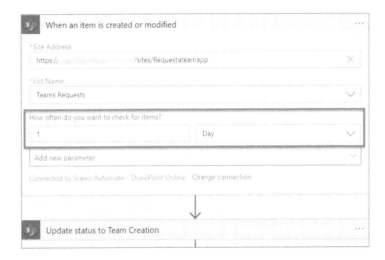

FIGURE 4.48
Logic App running in real time to provision new teams that have been approved

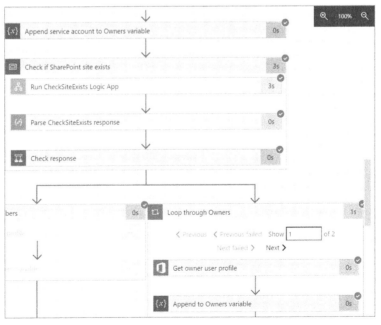

NOTE   To browse the Microsoft App Templates online gallery, please visit https://aka.ms/ TeamsAppTemplates.

FIGURE 4.49
Logic App Run history example showing a Running, Succeeded, and Failed process

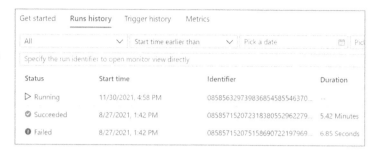

FIGURE 4.50
Email example sent to requestor from the Logic App

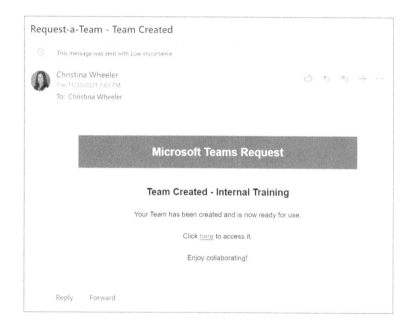

FIGURE 4.51
Newly created team shown that was auto provisioned by the Azure Logic App

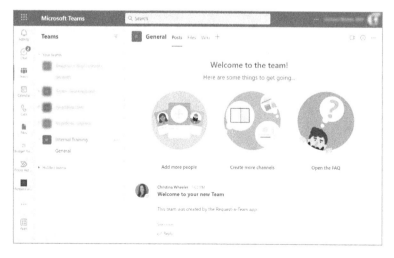

Power Platform (Low/No Code)

As you learned about in the Request A Team Power Platform solution and use case, the Power Platform can be extremely powerful to use within Teams. Microsoft has been investing heavily in Teams integration, and it recently released apps in Teams for Power Apps, Power Automate, Power Virtual Agents, and Power BI.

POWER APPS IN TEAMS

The Power Apps in Teams app enables you to create an app directly in Microsoft Teams that you can share with your teams. To work with Power Apps in Teams, you need to first install the app from the Teams app store. The app will be available for everyone to use, or you can also add it to a team or a chat (see Figure 4.52 and Figure 4.53).

FIGURE 4.52
Power Apps in Teams apps store and the home page for the app after it's installed

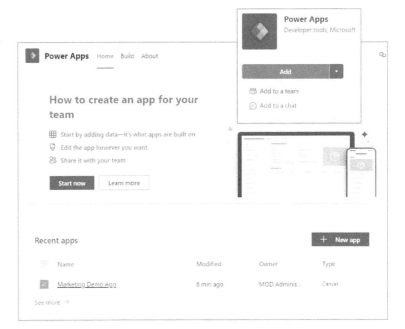

Create an App from Scratch

To create an app from scratch, you can click Start Now from the home page. You will then be prompted to choose a team you want to create the app in (see Figure 4.54). Clicking Create will redirect you to Power Apps Studio, which is part of the Build tab. You will be prompted to give your app a name (see Figure 4.55). From here, you can begin to build your app. You will have one screen with an empty canvas (see Figure 4.56). After you are done building your app in Power Apps Studio, you can publish it by clicking Publish To Teams (see Figure 4.57).

FIGURE 4.53
Screen after you choose the Add To A Team option when installing the app

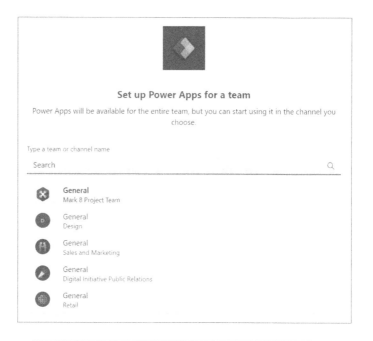

FIGURE 4.54
Selecting a team to create an app from scratch

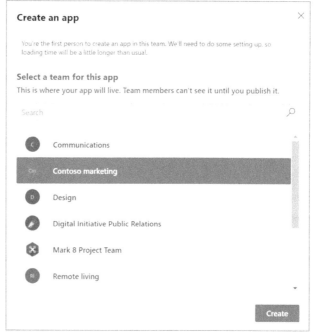

FIGURE 4.55
Name Your App

FIGURE 4.56
New app opened in
Power Apps Studio
inside of
Microsoft Teams

FIGURE 4.57
Publish To Teams button
for publishing your
app to Teams

Create an App from a Template

Another option you have is to add an app from one of the available templates (see Figure 4.58). For example, if you click Bulletins you will be prompted with the information for the app. To add, click Add To A Team (see Figure 4.59). Choose the team you want to create the app in, then click Set Up A Tab (see Figure 4.60). The app will create a new tab in your team called Bulletins and you will see a progress bar of the installation (see Figure 4.61).

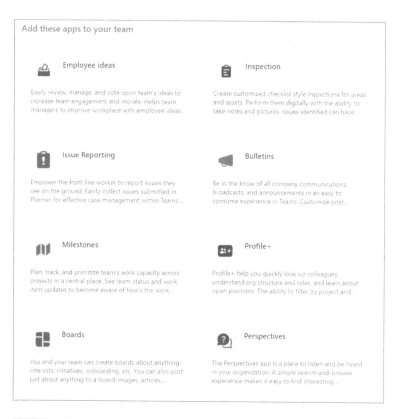

FIGURE 4.60
Set up Bulletins for a
team dialog where you
choose a team to
set up a tab

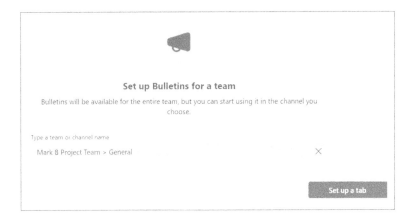

FIGURE 4.61
Bulletins installing the
app to the channel
progress showing in
Bulletins tab

Once the app is installed, you will see a dialog to grant access to any connections the app uses. For this example, the prompt is for Office 365 Users and Microsoft Stream (see Figure 4.62). By accepting consent, the Bulletins app will install and show up as a tab in the team (see Figure 4.63) with example postings (see Figure 4.64). You can click an example bulletin, delete the examples, or modify the existing examples to different content. When the app is installed, it also creates a tab called Manage Bulletins, which displays the admin screen of the Power App. On this screen, you can create and modify the bulletins for the app (see Figure 4.65).

NOTE   To learn more about the architecture and building apps using the Power Automate app in Microsoft Teams, please visit `https://docs.microsoft.com/en-us/powerapps/teams/create-apps-overview`.

FIGURE 4.62
Permissions consent
dialog for Bulletins app

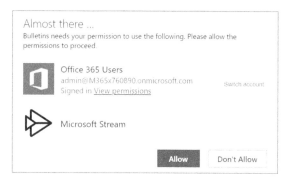

FIGURE 4.63
Bulletins app after
installation is complete

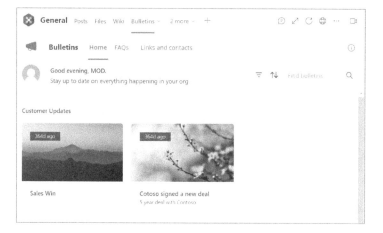

FIGURE 4.64
Example bulletin
displaying after clicking
bulletin item

FIGURE 4.65
Manage Bulletins tab displays the screen to create and modify bulletins

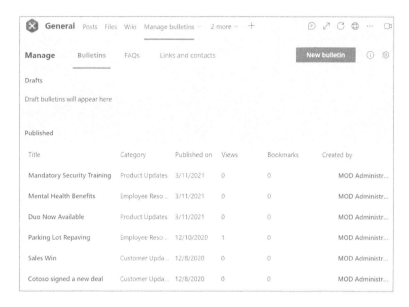

POWER AUTOMATE IN TEAMS

Power Automate is a no-code/low-code platform that allows users to automate repetitive tasks and business processes. You can create flows within the Power Automate service or with the Power Automate app in Microsoft Teams. Using the Power Automate app within Microsoft Teams allows you to create flows without needing to switch between multiple apps. To get started, you need to install the Power Automate app in the Teams apps store (see Figure 4.66). Once the app is added, you can create a flow from scratch by clicking + New Flow (see Figure 4.67) or choose from a variety of templates (see Figure 4.68). Some of the templates include:

- ◆ Post a welcome message when a new team member joins the team
- ◆ Schedule a meeting with a message sender
- ◆ Send a meeting reminder to Microsoft Teams during weekdays

FIGURE 4.66
Power Automate app in the Teams apps store

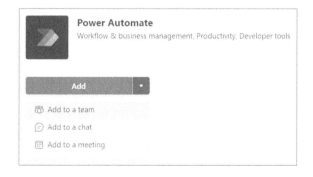

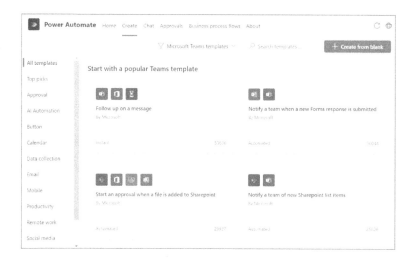

How Power Automate Works

Power Automate flows are based on *triggers* and *actions*. A trigger starts the flow, and an action is what happens once the flow is triggered. You can use triggers and actions specifically for Teams (see Figure 4.69) or trigger flows outside of Teams. For example, you can trigger a flow based on an email received with an attachment and have the flow's action copy the email into a SharePoint site document library for a team. You can also add multiple actions, so for this example you may also want to post a message in a Teams channel to let everyone know about the email that was uploaded.

NOTE To learn more about building flows using the Power Automate app in Microsoft Teams, please visit `https://docs.microsoft.com/en-us/power-automate/teams/overview`.

FIGURE 4.69
Triggers and Actions for
Microsoft Teams

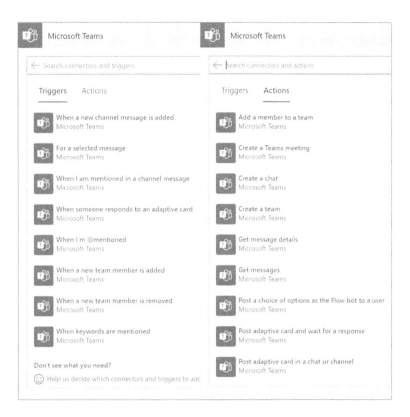

FIGURE 4.69
Triggers and Actions for
Microsoft Teams

POWER VIRTUAL AGENTS IN TEAMS

Power Virtual Agents is a way to create powerful chatbots that can answer questions asked by your users. Power Virtual Agents is available as a standalone web app and as an app in Microsoft Teams. You can add the Power Virtual Agents app from the Teams apps store (see Figure 4.70). A good use case for using Power Virtual Agents in Microsoft Teams is where you are an employee and want to create a chatbot to answer common questions asked by other members of your team (see Figure 4.71, Figure 4.72, Figure 4.73, and Figure 4.74).

FIGURE 4.70
Power Virtual Agents
app in Teams app store

FIGURE 4.71
Power Virtual Agents
app displaying in Teams

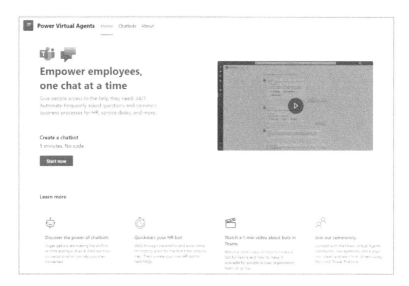

FIGURE 4.72
Create A Chatbot dialog
displaying example
teams for selecting a
team to create the
chatbot in

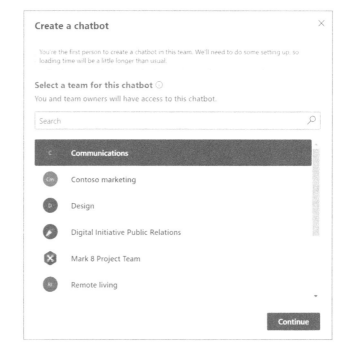

FIGURE 4.73
Testing Power Virtual
Agents chatbot in
Teams example

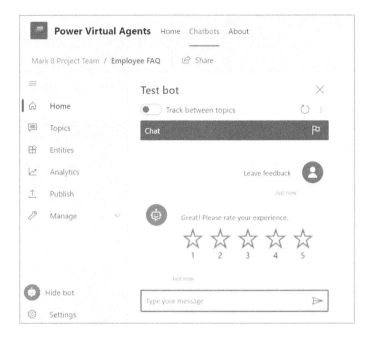

FIGURE 4.74
Employee FAQ example
Power Virtual
Agents chatbot

NOTE To learn more about the Power Virtual Agents app in Microsoft Teams, please visit
https://docs.microsoft.com/en-us/power-virtual-agents/teams/
fundamentals-what-is-power-virtual-agents-teams.

POWER BI FOR MICROSOFT TEAMS

The Power BI app in Teams is a great way to collaborate and analyze data directly within Microsoft Teams. The app in Microsoft Teams is your personal experience, which allows you to surface Power BI without having to get outside of Teams. After you install the app (see Figure 4.75), you can do almost everything in Microsoft Teams that you can do through the Power BI service (see Figure 4.76):

◆ Create, view, and edit dashboards, reports, and apps directly within the Power BI app in Microsoft Teams.

◆ Create and participate in workspaces directly within the app.

◆ Share content to others within Microsoft Teams.

FIGURE 4.75
Power BI app in the Teams apps store

FIGURE 4.76
Power BI app in Teams displaying the default home screen

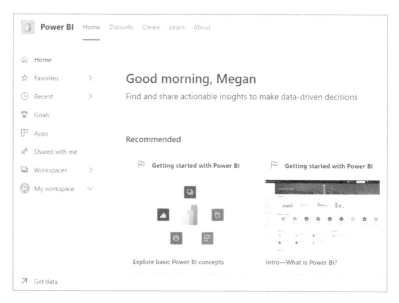

One of my favorite features with the Power BI app in Teams is the ability to generate a Power BI report to analyze your Microsoft Teams activity, in Teams. This report is personal to you, where only you can see the report and your Teams activity, unless you decide to share it. To generate the report, you need to open the Power BI app in Teams. Once open, click the Create tab and then select Analyze Your Teams Data (see Figure 4.77).

FIGURE 4.77
Power BI Create
tab in Teams

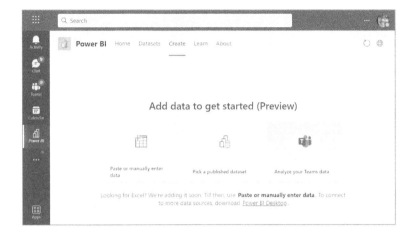

Power BI automatically creates your report, which gets saved to your My Workspace hosted in the Power BI Service. The report displays in the Power BI app within Teams personally for you (see Figure 4.78). The My Activity page shows a summary of your recent activity in Teams. The default time period is the past 31 days; however you can change the filter to show 7, 14, or 90 days instead.

FIGURE 4.78
Teams activity analytics
for My Activity example
report in the Power BI
app in Microsoft Teams

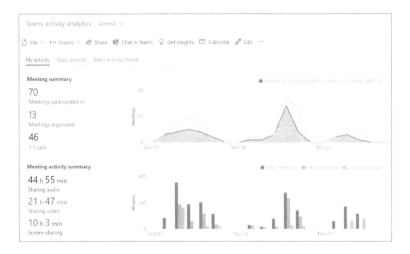

There's also a see a Team Activity link, which will take you to a Team Activity page. This page will show activity (such as # of posts, replies, active users, and guests) of all the teams you're a member of. If you want to drill down to more details of a team, you can click Team Activity Details as shown in Figure 4.79. You can also do other things with your report such as edit it, save a copy of the report, or download the .pbix file to edit in Power BI Desktop.

FIGURE 4.79
Team Activity Details
displaying in report

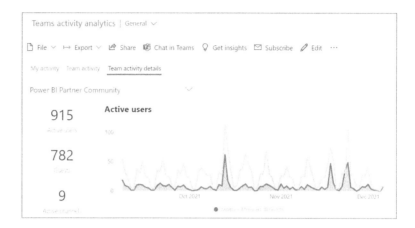

NOTE To learn more about the Power BI app in Microsoft Teams, please visit `https://docs`
`.microsoft.com/en-us/power-bi/collaborate-share/service-microsoft-teams-app`.

Microsoft Teams App Development Platform

There are some use cases where organizations have a need to create their own custom apps for
Teams. If you're a developer, you can use the Microsoft Teams Toolkit to custom develop your
own Microsoft Teams apps from scratch. The Microsoft Teams Toolkit is available to install for
Visual Studio Code (see Figure 4.80 and Figure 4.81) and Visual Studio.

FIGURE 4.80
Teams Toolkit Install for
Visual Studio Code

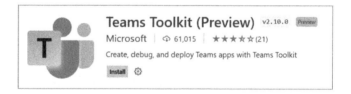

FIGURE 4.81
Visual Studio Code
Microsoft Teams Toolkit
landing page

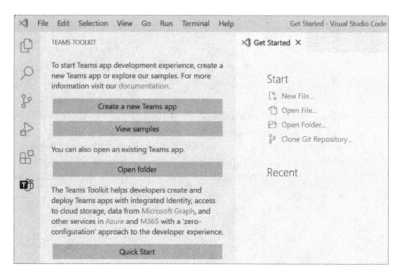

NOTE   To learn more about how to build custom apps for Microsoft Teams using Visual Studio Code or Visual Studio, please visit `https://docs.microsoft.com/en-us/microsoftteams/ platform/`.

The Bottom Line

Third-party Apps in Microsoft Teams.   Microsoft apps, third-party apps, and custom apps in Teams makes it easier for you to combine your core workloads with your other systems and processes outside of Microsoft Teams.

> **Master It**   Your organization is using ServiceNow for your IT support outside of Microsoft Teams. Any time someone needs help they open a ServiceNow ticket from the website, which requires IT engagement. You discover there are common issues users are asking about that can be easily addressed without IT's engagement and want a way for everyone to self-diagnose and remediate issues. If an issue can't be resolved, then a ticket can be open.

App Templates for Microsoft Teams.   App templates provide a great way to address business scenarios without having to develop an app for Teams from scratch. These low code/ no-code prebuilt templates are available online for free and can be implemented into your organizational tenant.

> **Master It**   Users are complaining they are unable to create a team. Your organization disabled all users from being able to create a team and only the highest-level admins can create teams. You want to put a process in place to allow users to request to have a team created and have the request go through an approval process. Once approved, you want the teams to be auto-provisioned.

Chapter 5

Administering Teams

Now that you have learned the basics of Teams, the next steps are to learn how to manage teams as an administrator using the Microsoft Teams admin center. Whether you're an administrator or not, it is beneficial to understand what settings you can set, which can help you and your organization decide on what features to enable or disable. Some organizations have administrators that handle all the Teams settings, while others may have several different types of Teams admins roles. In this chapter, you learn about the different roles to help you understand how your Teams can be managed as well as settings that you can change through the Microsoft Teams admin center. We will not cover all settings in this chapter, but we will cover the most used settings.

IN THIS CHAPTER, YOU WILL LEARN THE FOLLOWING

◆ Available Microsoft Teams administrator roles and settings in the Microsoft Teams admin center

◆ How to manage teams and templates

◆ Understanding policies and settings for meetings, messaging, and apps

◆ Understanding org-wide settings

◆ How to manage apps through permission and setup policies

◆ Microsoft Teams usage reports

Teams Administrator Roles

Teams can be managed through various role levels. Using Azure Active Directory (Azure AD), you can delegate administrators who need different levels of access for managing Microsoft Teams for your organization. Several Teams admin roles are available:

Teams administrator: Manage the Teams service, and manage and create Microsoft 365 Groups.

Teams communications administrator: Manage calling and meetings features within the Teams service.

Teams communications support engineer: Troubleshoot communications issues within Teams by using basic tools.

Teams communications support specialist: Troubleshoot communications issues within Teams using advanced tools.

Teams Device Administrator: Manage devices configured for use with the Teams service.

Teams Admin Center

Administrators can manage Teams through the Microsoft Teams admin center. The admin center provides a unified experience for managing Teams and Skype for Business. The dashboard is the default home page of the Teams admin center. It provides organization information, user search, user activity, release notes, training, and learn more resources section for the Teams Admin Center dashboard (see Figure 5.1). For full administration capabilities of the Teams admin center, you must have one of the following roles assigned:

◆ Global Administrator

◆ Teams Administrator

FIGURE 5.1
Microsoft Teams admin center dashboard default home page

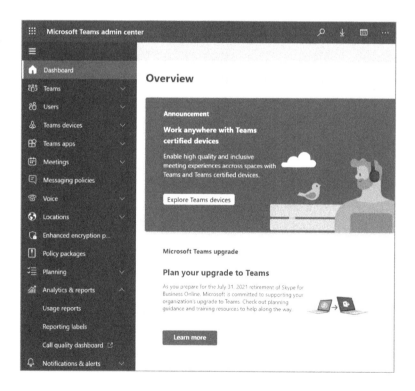

Teams Menu

The Teams menu in the Microsoft Teams admin center provides links to manage teams, teams policies, and templates (see Figure 5.2).

FIGURE 5.2
Teams menu options in
Microsoft Teams
admin center

MANAGE TEAMS

The Manage Teams page has a Users Summary count tile and a scrollable grid listing all teams that exist in your tenant (see Figure 5.3). The grid displays the following properties:

Team name: The name of your team

Channels: Count of all channels in the team (including the default General channel)

Team members: Count of total users (including owners, guests, and members)

Owners: Count of owners for the team

Guests: Count of Azure Active Directory B2B guest users who are members of the team

Privacy: Visibility/access type of the team backed by the Microsoft 365 group

Status: Archived or Active status for the team

Description: Description of the team backed by the Microsoft 365 group

Classification: Classification (if used in your organization) assigned backed by the Microsoft 365 group

Group ID: A Unique GroupID backed by the Microsoft 365 group

When you click a team to manage, it will open a page with more information about the team including a grid for Members, Channels, and Settings (see Figure 5.4).

Members

The Members grid shows the list of people that are members of the team. From this grid you can add new members by clicking the Add button or remove members by selecting a member (see Figure 5.5) and clicking the Remove button.

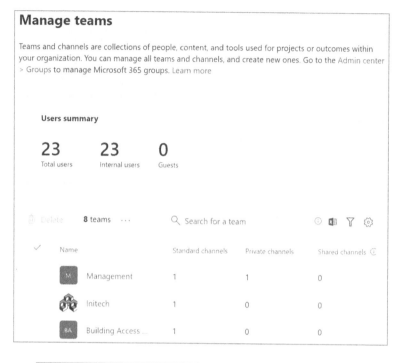

Manage teams

Teams and channels are collections of people, content, and tools used for projects or outcomes within your organization. You can manage all teams and channels, and create new ones. Go to the Admin center > Groups to manage Microsoft 365 groups. Learn more

Users summary

23	23	0
Total users	Internal users	Guests

🗑 Delete   **8 teams**   ···   🔍 Search for a team   ⓘ 📇 ▽ ⚙

	Name	Standard channels	Private channels	Shared channels ⓘ
	M Management	1	1	0
	🏢 Initech	1	0	0
	BA Building Access …	1	0	0

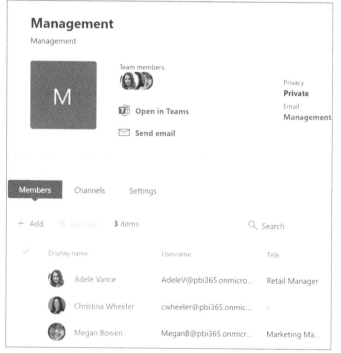

Management

Management

M

Team members

🎁 **Open in Teams**

✉ **Send email**

Privacy
Private

Email
Management

Members	Channels	Settings

➕ Add   ✕ Remove   **3 items**   🔍 Search

	Display name	Username	Title
	Adele Vance	AdeleV@pbi365.onmicro…	Retail Manager
	Christina Wheeler	cwheeler@pbi365.onmic…	-
	Megan Bowen	MeganB@pbi365.onmicr…	Marketing Ma…

FIGURE 5.5
Example with member selected that can be removed by clicking the Remove button

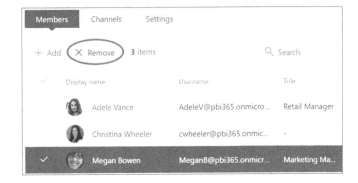

To add a member, click the + Add button and search for the user you want to add, and then click the user to add them to the list. Note: you can add up to 20 users at a time. Once you have added all the users you want, click Apply (see Figure 5.6). You can change the role of a user by selecting the Member drop-down and choosing Owner or Member (see Figure 5.7).

FIGURE 5.6
Searching for and adding a member to a team

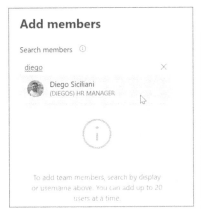
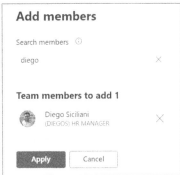

FIGURE 5.7
Changing user's role to Owner

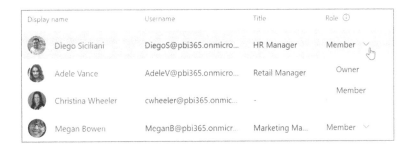

Channels

The Channels grid allows you to edit existing channels or add new channels within a team (see Figure 5.8). To add a new channel, click + Add and then give the channel a Name, a Description (optional), and set the Type to Standard or Private (see Figure 5.9). Private will only be available if private channels are allowed on the team you're adding the new channel to.

FIGURE 5.8
List of channels

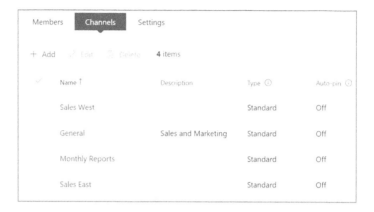

FIGURE 5.9
Adding a new channel
panel displaying
drop-down of
channel types

Settings

For each team, you can change the default Conversations and Channels settings (see Figure 5.10), such as not allowing users to edit or delete messages after they have been sent in conversations. You may not want members to be able to add/edit channels or add/edit/remove tabs. Additional settings include turning on/off the ability to add/edit/remove connectors, apps, and private channels.

Teams Policies

The Teams Policies page (see Figure 5.11) is where you can use teams and channel policies to control what settings or features are available to users when they are using teams and channels. For example, you can decide if your users are allowed to create private channels.

Members
Channels
Settings
Message permissions
Edit sent messages
On
Delete sent messages
On
Team owners can delete sent messages
On
Add and edit channels
On
Add and edit private channels
On
Delete channels
On
Add, edit, or remove tabs
On
Add, edit, or remove connectors
On
Add, edit, or remove apps
On
Mentions
Mention teams in messages
On
Mention channels in messages
On
Guest permissions
Guests can add and edit channels
Off
Guests can delete channels
Off
Fun settings
Giphy
On
Giphy content rating
Strict
Stickers and memes
On
Custom memes
On

FIGURE 5.10 Settings for modifying a team

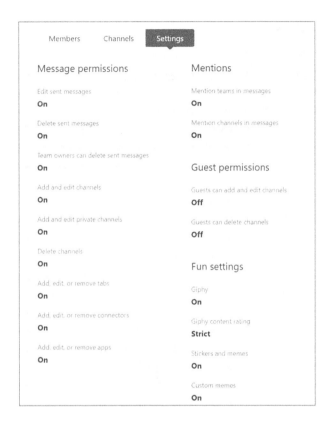

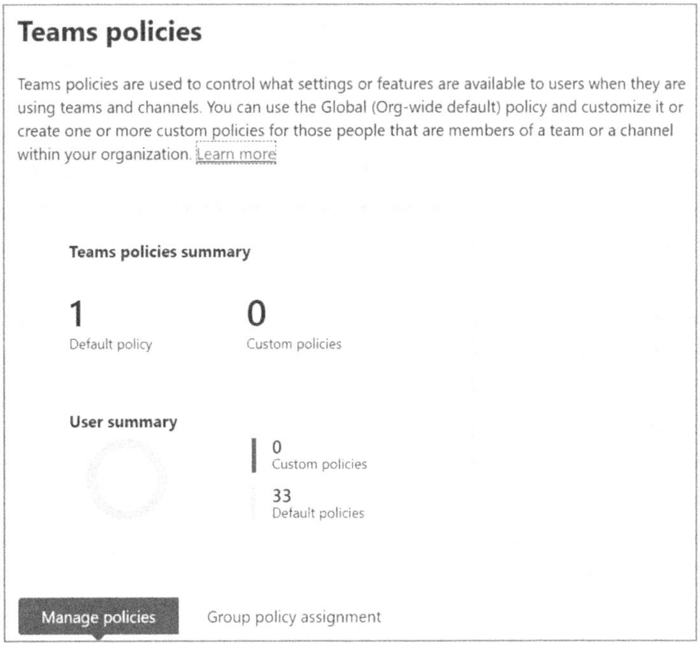
Teams policies
Teams policies are used to control what settings or features are available to users when they are using teams and channels. You can use the Global (Org-wide default) policy and customize it or create one or more custom policies for those people that are members of a team or a channel within your organization. Learn more
Teams policies summary
1
Default policy
0
Custom policies
User summary
0
Custom policies
33
Default policies
Manage policies
Group policy assignment

FIGURE 5.11 Teams Policies settings page

MANAGING POLICIES

All tenants will have a Global (Org-Wide Default) policy that you can use or customize, or you can create one or more custom policies and manage users for each of the custom policies (see Figure 5.12). To create a custom policy, click + Add, set the values, and then click Apply (see Figure 5.13).

FIGURE 5.12
Manage Policies grid
displaying default policy

FIGURE 5.13
New teams policy
example disallowing
creation of private
channels

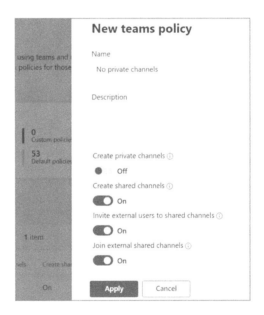

GROUP POLICY ASSIGNMENT

After you create one or more custom Teams policies, you can assign individual users to each policy. Instead of assigning each user individually you can assign groups to your custom policies under the Group Policy Assignment settings (see Figure 5.14). To assign a group to a policy, click + Add Group, set the values, and then click Apply (see Figure 5.15).

FIGURE 5.14
Group Policy
Assignment grid with
example custom policy

FIGURE 5.15
Assigning a group to a
custom policy

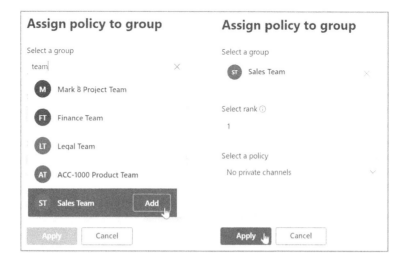

Update Policies

Update Polices is where you manage the Teams and Office preview features for users to see pre-release or preview features in the Teams app within your organization. The Global (Org-Wide Default) policy is set to Follow Office Preview by default (see Figure 5.16). You can leave this setting as is, change the default policy to Not Enabled or Enabled (see Figure 5.17), or you can create your own custom update policy.

Teams Templates

Teams comes with a set of pre-built templates designed around a business need or project (see Figure 5.18). These templates come with predefined channels and apps, and can be assigned to a specific group using team policies.

FIGURE 5.16
Teams Update Policies
settings page

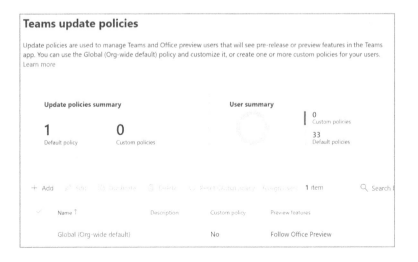

Teams update policies

Update policies are used to manage Teams and Office preview users that will see pre-release or preview features in the Teams app. You can use the Global (Org-wide default) policy and customize it, or create one or more custom policies for your users. Learn more

Update policies summary		User summary	
1	**0**		0 Custom policies
Default policy	Custom policies		33 Default policies

+ Add	Edit	Duplicate	Delete	Reset Global policy	Assigned users	1 item	Q Search

✓	Name ↑	Description	Custom policy	Preview features
	Global (Org-wide default)		No	Follow Office Preview

FIGURE 5.17
Drop-down options for
the Show Preview
Features property

Update policy

Name

Global

Description

Show preview features

Follow Office Preview ⌄

Not enabled

Enabled

Follow Office Preview

CREATING NEW TEMPLATES

You can create new templates easily through the Create A Template wizard. When creating a new template, you will be given options to set as a starting point (see Figure 5.19). These options include:

- ◆ Create A New Template
- ◆ Use An Existing Team As A Template
- ◆ Start With An Existing Template

FIGURE 5.18
Some of the predefined
team templates

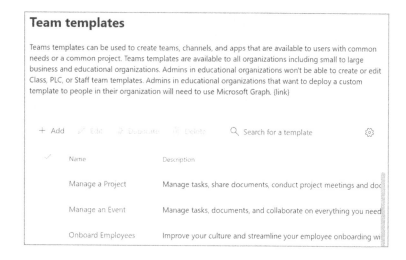

FIGURE 5.19
Create A Template
wizard with the starting
point options

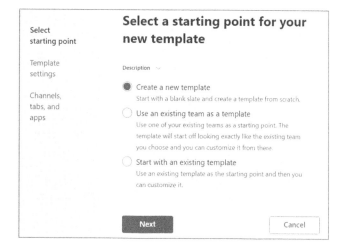

NOTE Custom templates are not yet supported for EDU customers. To read more and to learn about known issues, please visit https://docs.microsoft.com/en-us/microsoftteams/create-a-team-template.

Template Policies

You can hide/show templates assigned to the default policy, and you can also create custom policies. It is best practice for organizations to hide pre-built templates that don't apply to their business. For example, if your organization is not a hospital or a retail store, you may want to hide the pre-built templates by selecting the ones you do not want to use and then click Hide (see

Figure 5.20). After you click Hide, the templates will show up under the Hidden Templates grouping (Figure 5.21). You can preview the list of templates you want to hide, and then click Save.

FIGURE 5.20
Hiding pre-built hospital and retail scenario templates

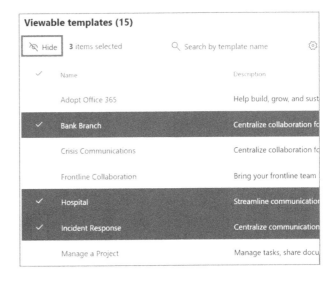

FIGURE 5.21
Hidden templates

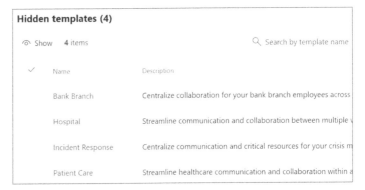

Meetings Menu

The Meetings menu is where you can manage settings for conference bridges, meeting policies/settings, and live events policies/settings.

Conference Bridges

Even if you do not have audio conferencing licenses purchased and assigned to users, you will see the conference bridges settings in the Microsoft Teams admin center. With Audio Conferencing, your users can use toll and toll-free phone numbers so attendees can dial in to meetings. Toll (service) numbers are automatically assigned as shared audio-conferencing numbers to organizations when enabled for Audio Conferencing. Dedicated toll and toll-free numbers can be assigned to your organization from additional cities. If you decide you want Audio Conferencing for your organization, you will need to purchase one Audio Conferencing license for each person in your organization who will schedule/host audio meetings.

NOTE Toll-free (service) phone numbers are only available in some countries/regions. To see what is available in your country or region, please visit `https://docs.microsoft.com/en-US/ microsoftteams/country-and-region-availability-for-audio-conferencing- and-calling-plans/country-and-region-availability-for-audio-conferencing- and-calling-plans`.

Two types of audio-conferencing phone numbers can be assigned to your conferencing bridge:

Dedicated: Dedicated phone numbers are available only to users within your organization.

Shared: Shared phone numbers are not dedicated, and you can't change the languages used when someone calls in to one of these numbers.

Meeting Policies

Meeting policies (see Figure 5.22) contain settings to control what features are available to users when they join meetings. There are six default policies, including a Global (Org-Wide Default) policy, which you can customize, or you can create your own custom meeting policies.

FIGURE 5.22
Meeting Policies
landing page

MANAGING POLICIES

The Manage Policies grid contains six default polices (see Figure 5.23) called AllOn, RestrictedAnonymousAccess, AllOff, RestrictedAnonymousNoRecording, Kiosk, and Global (Org-Wide Default). You cannot delete any of these default policies and you can only edit the Global (Org-Wide Default) policy. .

FIGURE 5.23
Manage Policies showing
the six default polices

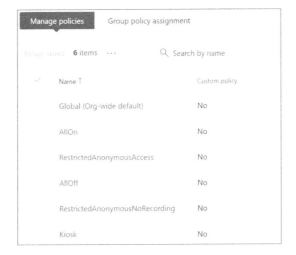

General

You can create new policies or update exiting policies. When you create or update existing policies you will have different sections of settings you can modify. The General section provides settings for allowing/disallowing Meet Now in channels, Outlook add-in, channel meeting scheduling, scheduling private meetings, engagement report, meeting registration, and who is allowed to register (see Figure 5.24).

FIGURE 5.24
General section settings
for meeting policies

General		^
These are the general settings for meeting policies. Learn more		
Meet now in channels	On	
Outlook add-in	On	
Channel meeting scheduling	On	
Private meeting scheduling	On	
Engagement report ⓘ	Turn on	⌄
Webinar registration ⓘ	On	
Who can register ⓘ	Everyone	⌄

The Allow Engagement Report setting allows your organizers to see who registered and attended the meetings and webinars they scheduled. All Meeting Registration allows users to schedule webinars. The Who Can Register setting is set to Everyone by default, which means all users (including anonymous users) can register and attend webinars. You can change this setting to Everyone In Company to only allow users in your organization to register for webinars, or if you want to disable webinars you can set Allow Meeting Registration to Off.

Audio & Video

Under the Audio & Video section are settings where you can turn on/off transcriptions for meetings, cloud recording, mode for IP audio/video, IP video, and NDI streaming, and you can change the value of the Media Bit Rate (KBS) (see Figure 5.25). If your organization does not want any meetings to be recorded, you will need to set Allow Cloud Recording to Off.

FIGURE 5.25
Audio & Video default
meeting policy settings

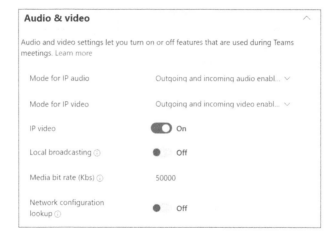

Broadcast Audio and Video from Teams with NDI Technology

NewTek NDI (Network Device Interface) technology is a standard industry solution for producing live content for streams. NDI allows you to connect media devices such as a studio camera and mixer. Instead of using physical connections, NDI technology enables connectivity over a local intranet on a local machine.

NOTE   To learn more about using NDI with Teams, please visit `https://docs.microsoft.com/en-US/microsoftteams/use-ndi-in-meetings`.

Recording and Transcription

The Recording & Transcription section (see Figure 5.26) is where you can enable or disable transcription, cloud recording, recording expiration, storing recordings outside of your country or region. Many organizations leave transcription off however may want to considering enabling this feature. Transcription is helpful so users can play back the meeting with closed captions.

FIGURE 5.26
Recording and
Transcription settings

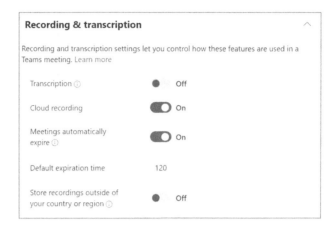

Recording & transcription ∧

Recording and transcription settings let you control how these features are used in a Teams meeting. Learn more

Transcription ⓘ	⬤ Off	
Cloud recording	⬤ On	
Meetings automatically expire ⓘ	⬤ On	
Default expiration time	120	
Store recordings outside of your country or region ⓘ	⬤ Off	

Content Sharing

The Content Sharing section contains settings for controlling the different types of content that can be used during Teams meetings held within your organization (see Figure 5.27). By default, participants within your organization can give or request control, but external participants cannot. In certain situations you may want to turn on Allow An External Participant To Give Or Request Control, such as when you have people outside of your organization providing technical support.

FIGURE 5.27
Content Sharing settings

Content sharing ∧

Content sharing settings let you control the different types of content that can be used during Teams meetings that are held in your organization. Learn more

Screen sharing mode	Entire screen	∨
Participants can give or request control	⬤ On	
External participants can give or request control	⬤ Off	
PowerPoint Live	⬤ On	
Whiteboard	⬤ On	
Shared notes ⓘ	⬤ On	
Select video filters Video filters aren't available for all Teams clients. Learn more	All filters	∨

Other settings you can change are PowerPoint sharing, whiteboard, shared notes, and video filters. The Select Video Filters setting is set to All Filters by default, but you can change this to No Filter, Background Blur Only, or Background Blur And Default Images (see Figure 5.28). Table 5.1 describes each mode.

FIGURE 5.28
Select Video Filters
drop-down options

Select video filters		
Video filters aren't available for all Teams clients. Learn more	All filters	⌄
	No filter	
	Background blur only	
	Background blur and default images	
		⌃
	All filters	

TABLE 5.1   Video Filters Mode

MODE	BEHAVIOR
No Filter	Users can't customize their video background.
Background Blur Only	Users have the option to blur their video background.
Background Blur And Default Images	Users have the option to blur their background or choose from the default set of images as their background. They cannot upload custom backgrounds.
All Filters	This is the default setting that allows users to blur their video background, choose a set of default images, or upload custom images to use as their background.

NOTE   When you use the All Filters setting, images uploaded by your users are not screened by Teams. It is recommended you have internal organizational policies to prevent users from uploading/ using offensive or inappropriate images.

For more details on Content Sharing settings, please visit `https://docs.microsoft.com/en-us/ microsoftteams/meeting-policies-content-sharing`.

Participants & Guests

The Participants & Guests settings let you control the default settings for your Teams meetings (see Figure 5.29). You can control if anonymous users can start a meeting, change what roles have presenter rights, who you want to allow to automatically be admitted into meetings, allow dial-in users to bypass the lobby, meet now in private meetings, enable live captions, and allow chat in meetings. Live transcription is turned off by default, but you may want to enable it if you have participants who are deaf or hard-of-hearing. Transcription can also be helpful in situations when you have different levels of language proficiency or for participants who are attending meetings from noisy places.

FIGURE 5.29
Participants &
Guests settings

NOTE Meeting participants can choose to not be identified in meeting transcriptions when attending. Live transcription cannot be viewed by attendees who call in using a dial-in number, and other limitations exist. To learn more about live transcription, current limitations, settings, and how to not be identified, please visit `https://support.microsoft.com/en-us/office/view-live-transcription-in-a-teams-meeting-dc1a8f23-2e20-4684-885e--2152e06a4a8b`.

For more details on IP audio and IP video settings, please visit `https://docs.microsoft.com/en-us/microsoftteams/meeting-policies-audio-and-video#video-filters-mode`.

Meeting Settings

The meeting settings are used to control whether anonymous users can join Teams meetings (see Figure 5.30), what to include in email invitations for Teams meetings, as well as network settings to enable Quality of Service (QoS) and set ports for real-time traffic.

FIGURE 5.30
Meeting Settings page
with the anonymous
setting for participants

Meeting settings

Meeting settings are used to control whether anonymous people can join Teams meetings and what is included in the meeting invitations. You can also enable Quality of Service (QoS) and set the ports for real-time traffic. These settings are used for all Teams meetings that people schedule in your organization. Learn more

Participants

Anonymous users can join a meeting   On

Anonymous users can interact with apps in meetings   On

EMAIL INVITATION SETTINGS

Teams provides the option to set a logo, legal text, help link, and footer text for the email invitations for your Teams meetings (see Figure 5.31). For example, you can set the logo and footer text then click Preview Invite to preview the email invitation (see Figure 5.32).

FIGURE 5.31
Email Invitation settings

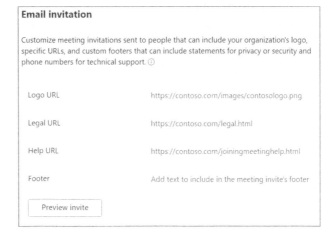

FIGURE 5.32
Email Invite
Preview example

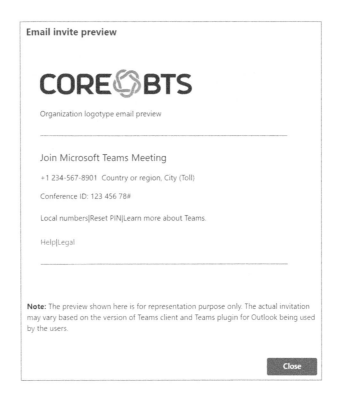

Live Events

The live events settings you can control in the Microsoft Teams admin center are live events policies and org-wide settings.

LIVE EVENT POLICIES

Microsoft Teams live events policies are where you can configure and manage settings such as who can join a live event, if recording is available for people who schedule and hold live events, and if transcription will be provided for attendees. You can use the Global (Org-Wide Default) policy (see Figure 5.33), customize it, or create additional policies with different settings and assign them to people within your organization who hold live events.

FIGURE 5.33
Global (Org-Wide
Default) policy settings

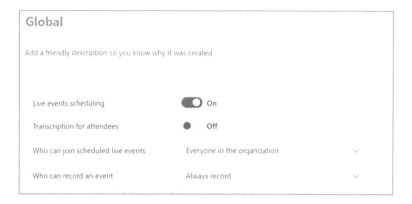

The default setting for who can join scheduled live events is Everyone In The Organization; however, if you want to open it to allow people outside your organization, set it to Everyone. You also have the option to choose Specific Users Or Groups within your organization to target individual users (see Figure 5.34). Who can record an event defaults to Always Record, which you can change to Never Record or to Organizer Can Record (see Figured 5.35).

FIGURE 5.34
Who can join scheduled
live events drop-down
menu options

FIGURE 5.35
Who can record an event
drop-down
menu options

Record an event	Organizer can record	∨
	Always record	
	Never record	
Save Cancel	Organizer can record	

LIVE EVENT SETTINGS

If your organization uses a third-party video distribution provider, also known as enterprise content delivery network (eCDN), such as Hive or Kollective for all live events, you can set it up in the Live Events Settings page (see Figured 5.36).

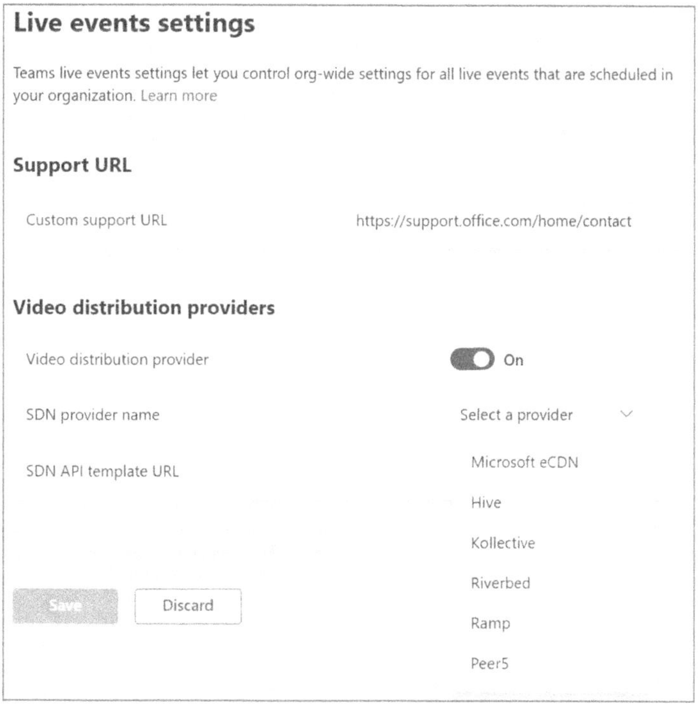

FIGURE 5.36
Live Event Settings showing drop-down menu options for third-party distribution provider

Live events settings

Teams live events settings let you control org-wide settings for all live events that are scheduled in your organization. Learn more

Support URL

Custom support URL   https://support.office.com/home/contact

Video distribution providers

Video distribution provider   On

SDN provider name   Select a provider   ⌄

SDN API template URL   Microsoft eCDN

                                                    Hive

                                                    Kollective

                                                    Riverbed

Save   Discard   Ramp

                                                    Peer5

Messaging Policies Menu

Messaging policies (see Figure 5.37) are settings where you can control chat and channel messaging features available to users in Microsoft Teams. There is a Global (Org-Wide Default) policy you can use or modify, or you can create new custom messaging policies. You can control if owners can delete sent messages by users in a team, control if users can delete sent messages, delete chat, edit sent messages, and set the default behavior for read receipts for all teams (see Figure 5.38).

There is an option to completely disable chat, however it is not common for organizations to disable it. You can also control if giphy, memes, and stickers are allowed in chats. If you allow giphy, you can change the restriction level. The default rating setting is set to Moderate; however, you can change it to Strict or No Restriction (see Figure 5.39). It is not recommended to use No Restriction. Voice messages are enabled by default for chats and channels but can be disabled or restricted to chat only (see Figure 5.40).

FIGURE 5.37
Messaging Policies
settings page

Messaging policies

Messaging policies are used to control what chat and channel messaging features are available to users in Teams. You can use the Global (Org-wide default) policy or create one or more custom messaging policies for people in your organization. Learn more

Messaging policies summary

1	0
Default policy	Custom policies

User summary

0
Custom policies

33
Default policies

Manage policies	Group policy assignment

↻ Reset Global policy   Assign users   1 item   ···   🔍 Search by name   ⚙

✓	Name ↑	Description	Custom policy
✓	Global (Org-wide default)		No

FIGURE 5.38
Global (Org-Wide
Default) policy settings
showing drop-down
options for read receipts

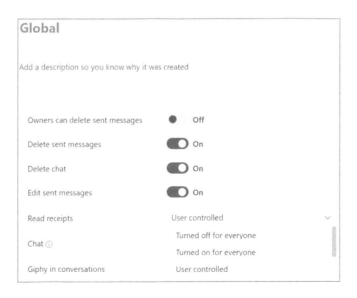

Global

Add a description so you know why it was created

Owners can delete sent messages	● Off
Delete sent messages	🔵 On
Delete chat	🔵 On
Edit sent messages	🔵 On
Read receipts	User controlled ⌄
	Turned off for everyone
Chat ⓘ	Turned on for everyone
Giphy in conversations	User controlled

FIGURE 5.39
Additional policy
settings showing
drop-down options for
Giphy Content Rating

FIGURE 5.40
Additional policy
settings showing
drop-down options for
Create Voice Messages

Users Menu

The Users menu contains all the settings for managing users, external access, and guest access.

Guest Access and External Access

When you need to communicate and collaborate with people outside your organization, Teams has two options:

External access: Type of federation that allows users to find, call, and chat with people in other organizations. External users cannot be added to teams unless they are invited as guests.

Guest access: Allows you to invite people from outside your organization to join a team.

Many organizations do not understand how guest access and external access work, and due to security concerns, admins often disable both. By disabling external access, organizations cripple themselves from being able to communicate with anyone outside their organization. It is important to understand how both guest and external access works so you can make a better decision to decide if you want to leave these settings on or disable them.

NOTE   Teams allows you to invite people outside your organization to meetings and does not require external or guest access to be configured.

EXTERNAL ACCESS (FEDERATION)

External access enables you to communicate with users outside of your organization within Teams. It connects your Office 365 tenant to another tenant to allow your users to find, call, and chat with external users who are not part of your organization. If this is disabled, your users will not be able to communicate through Teams with external users. They can invite them to meetings but will not be able to find them in Teams to chat with or call directly outside of a scheduled meeting.

GUEST ACCESS

Guest access is different than external access. With guest access enabled, you can add users outside of your organization as guests to teams, chats, channels, documents, resources, and applications. A guest is someone who isn't a member (such as an employee or student) within your organization. Some examples of guests may include partners, vendors, consultants, or suppliers. When guest access is enabled, anyone who is not part of your organization can be added as a guest in Teams. This means anyone with a business account (Azure Active Directory account) or consumer email account (Outlook.com, Gmail.com, or others) can participate as a guest in Teams providing access to teams and channel experiences.

NOTE   The guest experience has limitations by design. For a full list of the limitations and a comparison of what guests can and can't do, please visit https://docs.microsoft.com/en-us/microsoftteams/guest-experience#comparison-of-team-member-and-guest-capabilities.

If you only want to be able to find, call, and chat with people outside of your organization without allowing them to be added as guests to teams, use external access.

Teams Settings

Teams settings is where you can configure settings such as notifications, tagging, email integration, cloud file storage options, the Organization tab, Surface Hub device settings, the Exchange address book policy for how search operates in Microsoft Teams, and role-based chat permissions.

NOTIFICATIONS AND FEEDS

By default, suggested and trending feeds are enabled to appear in a user's activity feed (see Figure 5.41). You can disable suggested feeds simply by turning the toggle off in the Teams settings page.

FIGURE 5.41
Notifications and
Feeds toggle

Notifications and feeds

Manage the way that Teams handles suggested and trending feeds.

Suggested feeds can appear in a user's activity feed   On

TAGGING

Tagging is a feature in Teams that allows you to categorize people based on attributes such as role, skill, project, training, or location. Tags enable you to reach groups of people in Teams without having to type every single name. Once a tag is added, just @mention the tag in a channel. Everyone who has been assigned the tag will receive a notification just as they would if they were @mentioned individually. Another way to use a tag is to start a new chat and select the tag that is assigned to the people you want to reach.

Managing Custom Tags for Your Organization

As an admin, you can control how tags are used and managed across your organization through the Tagging settings (see Figure 5.42) in the Microsoft Teams admin center. The default setting for Tags Are Managed By is Team Owners. You can use the drop-down menu to change that setting to Team Owners And Members (see Figure 5.43) or to Not Enabled.

FIGURE 5.42
Tagging settings that can be set under your Teams settings

Tagging

Tags can be added to one or more team members and used to communicate with tagged with those members using @mentions of the tag in a channel post or starting a chat conversation. Learn more

Who can manage tags ⓘ	Team owners ⌄
Team owners can change who can manage tags ⓘ	🔘 On
Suggested tags ⓘ	
Press the space bar after you enter a tag.	
Custom tags ⓘ	🔘 On
Shifts app can apply tags ⓘ	🔘 On

FIGURE 5.43
Tags are managed by drop-down options

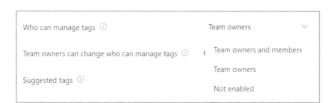

Who can manage tags ⓘ	Team owners ⌄
Team owners can change who can manage tags ⓘ	Team owners and members
	Team owners
Suggested tags ⓘ	Not enabled

Email Integration

The Email Integration setting is for allowing or disallowing users to send emails to a channel email address. By default, this setting is enabled but you have the option to disable it, and you can also specify SMTP domains you only want to accept channel emails from (see Figure 5.44).

FIGURE 5.44
Email
Integration settings

Files

The Files settings allows you to turn on/off file sharing and cloud file storage options for Citrix, DropBox, Box, Google Drive, and Egnyte (see Figure 5.45).

FIGURE 5.45
Cloud file storage
options that you can
turn on or off

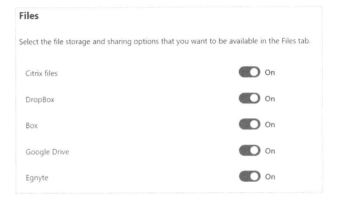

Organization

The Organization setting allows you to enable or disable (see Figure 5.46) users from seeing the Organization icon and tab so users can see others in their organization hierarchy (see Figure 5.47). This setting will hide the organization hierarchy in Teams that presents your manager or direct reports.

FIGURE 5.46
Show Organization Tab
In Chats toggle setting

Devices

The Devices setting is for controlling the resource account settings for Surface Hub devices attending Teams meetings (see Figure 5.48).

FIGURE 5.47
Organization icon and
tab example

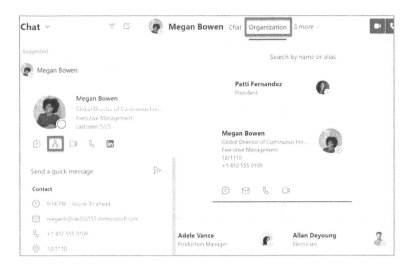

FIGURE 5.48
Devices default settings
for Surface Hub devices

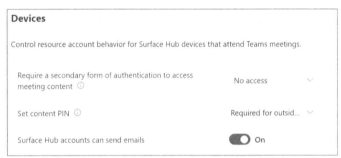

Search By Name

Search By Name is disabled by default (see Figure 5.49). You can enable this setting if you want the scope of the directory search to use the Exchange address book policy. It is common to leave this setting turned off.

FIGURE 5.49
Search By Name
default setting

Safety and Communications

The Safety And Communications setting is also turned off by default (see Figure 5.50). You can enable this setting if you want to turn on role-based chat permission for your organization. It is not common to turn this on, but if you do enable it you want to ensure chat is turned on for each user and that they have the correct chat permissions role assigned.

FIGURE 5.50
Role-Based Chat
Permissions setting

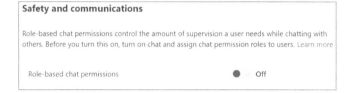

Teams Apps Menu

The Teams Apps menu provides settings to manage apps, permission policies, setup policies, and to customize the Teams apps store.

Manage Apps

By default, the tenant will be enabled to allow third-party apps and custom apps. These settings can be changed at the Teams tenant level by the admin. To check the settings, navigate to the Teams admin center (https://admin.teams.microsoft.com). In the left navigation menu, select Manage Apps and click the Org-Wide App Settings button (see Figure 5.51). A panel will display toggle settings for allowing and disallowing third-party apps and custom apps (see Figure 5.52).

FIGURE 5.51
Org-Wide App
Settings button

The options available are:

Third-Party Apps: The first option, Allow Third-Party Apps, allows users to install third-party apps in Teams. The second option, Allow Any New Third-Party Apps Published To The Store By Default, enables users to install newly published apps when they show up in the app store.

Custom Apps: If you want to deploy app templates or your own custom developed apps for Teams, you must enable the feature Allow Interaction With Custom Apps.

It is recommended you keep these org-wide settings as is and instead control apps allowed or disallowed for Microsoft Teams through permission policies.

FIGURE 5.52
Org-Wide App
Settings panel

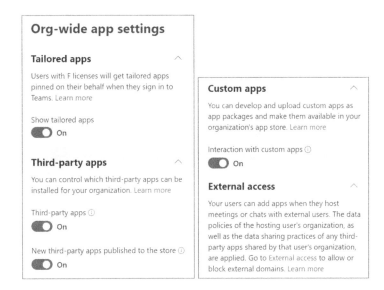

Permission Policies

Instead of disabling third-party and custom apps at the manage apps global level as shown previously in Figure 5.52, it is recommended you control app access through the app permission policies. App permission polices come with a default Global (Org-Wide Default) policy that you can use and modify, or create additional policies. It is common for organizations to lock down what apps they allow at the global level but then create a custom policy for IT admins, allowing them to use all apps so they can test and help determine what can be allowed for the rest of the organization (see Figure 5.54). The Global (Org-Wide Default) policy and any custom policy will have three drop-down settings for allowing or blocking Microsoft apps, third-party apps, and custom apps. By default, Allow All Apps is enabled, which Microsoft Teams administrators can change at any time (see Figure 5.55).

When Allow All Apps is enabled, this means that when users are logged in to Microsoft Teams they will see all Microsoft apps, third-party apps, and custom apps (if deployed) in the apps store (see Figure 5.56). The Built For Your Org category will show all custom apps available in the apps store. You should see two sections with one Built For Your Org (see Figure 5.57) and Built With Power Platform (see Figure 5.58).

Let's get back to the scenario of blocking at the global level but allowing at the IT admin level. To block at the global level, click the Global (Org-Wide Default) link (see Figure 5.59) to open the settings for the policy. In this case, your organization wants to allow Microsoft apps and custom apps deployed by your org, but block all third-party apps. To implement this setting, change the drop-down option to Block All Apps for the Third-Party Apps setting (see Figure 5.60). Once saved, when anyone within your organization logs in to Microsoft Teams and goes to the apps store, they will see only Microsoft apps available to choose from (see Figure 5.61). Note that the policy may take time to propagate for your users.

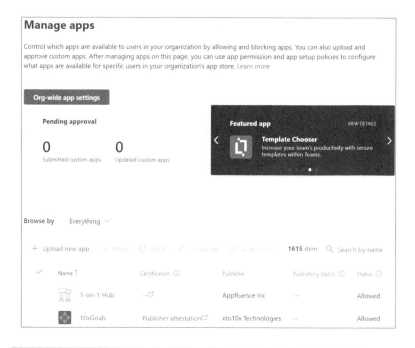

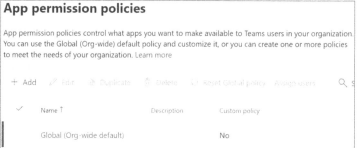

FIGURE 5.56
Microsoft Teams apps store displaying top picks third-party apps

FIGURE 5.57
Microsoft Teams apps store displaying Built for your org example apps

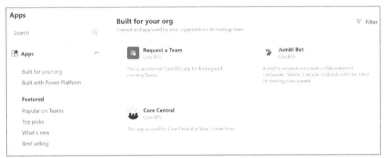

FIGURE 5.58
Microsoft Teams apps store displaying Built with Power Platform example apps

FIGURE 5.59
App Permission Policies settings showing Global (Org-Wide Default) link

FIGURE 5.60
Global policy highlight-
ing the third-party apps
policy change

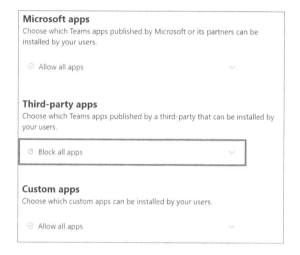

FIGURE 5.61
Apps store in Microsoft
Teams showing only
Microsoft apps
available for users

Setup Policies

The App Setup Policies page is where your Microsoft Teams administrator can control how apps are made available to a user or group of users within Microsoft Teams. Two policies are already created for you: the Global (Org-Wide Default) policy and the FirstLineWorker policy (see Figure 5.62). You can use the Global (Org-Wide Default) policy, customize it, or create additional app setup policies.

FIGURE 5.62
App Setup Policies page
showing default
setup policies

The setup policies settings you can configure are:

◆ **Pinned Apps**: You can choose apps to pin in the Microsoft Teams navigation bar for users in the setup policy. You can set the order in which they show up and control whether users can pin their own apps.

◆ **Installed Apps**: Install apps on behalf of users when they start Microsoft Teams and during meetings.

◆ **Upload Custom Apps**: Allow (or disallow) users to upload custom apps to Microsoft Teams.

A common scenario for organizations is to configure multiple setup policies targeted for specific users. For example, you may want to create a setup policy for human resources so when they log in to Microsoft Teams, they already have the Human Resources app installed and pinned on the navigation bar. To set this up, click + Add to create a new policy, give it a name, and then configure the Installed Apps (see Figure 5.63) and Pinned Apps settings (see Figure 5.64). The next step after creating a new setup policy is to assign users to the policy. Then, when any of the users assigned to the policy log in, they will see the newly installed and pinned app both in the client and mobile app (see Figure 5.65).

Customize Store

The Microsoft Teams apps store has default branding, which you can customize to use your company's branding. You can customize the store by adding your logo, custom text colors, and custom backgrounds to make it more inviting for your Microsoft Teams users. Microsoft Teams administrators can implement your company branding by selecting Teams Apps - Customize Store (see Figure 5.66).

Human Resources

Add a description so you know why it was created

Upload custom apps ⓘ   ● Off

User pinning ⓘ   ◯● On

Installed apps
Choose which apps and messaging extensions you want installed in your users' personal
Teams environment and in meetings they create. Users can install other available apps
from the Teams app store. Learn more

+ Add apps   ✕ Remove   **1** item

✓   Name   App ID

▣   Human Resources   1e4f1c34-7afd-44f4-b2e1-1edb6686e

Pinned apps
Choose the order apps are pinned in messaging extensions and the Teams app bar. Learn more

+ Add apps   ⬆ Move up   ⬇ Move down   ✕ Remove   **7** items

✓ App bar ⓘ   ✓ Messaging extensions ⓘ

1   ▣ Activity   =   ▣ Human Resources   =

2   ▣ Chat   =

3   ▣ Teams   =

4   ▣ Calendar   =

5   ▣ Calling   =

6   ▣ Files   =

CUSTOMIZE TO USE YOUR ORGANIZATION LOGO

In this option, you can upload your company logo so it will appear in Microsoft Teams in the
Apps ➤ Built For Your Org page in the top-right corner. When you select the Choose An Image
option, you can upload the file of your choice (see Figure 5.67 and Figure 5.68). The logo needs to
be 240×60 pixels, or it will be scaled to that size. The file size must be 5 MB or smaller and the
support formats are .svg, .png, and .jpg. Previewing the settings will show something similar
to Figure 5.69. Note that it can take up to 24 hours for your custom branding to appear in the
Microsoft Teams apps store.

FIGURE 5.65
Microsoft Teams
example showing where
apps can be pinned that
show in client and
mobile app

Desktop Teams App   iOS Teams App

FIGURE 5.66
Customize Store link
under the Teams apps
menu in the Microsoft
Teams admin center

FIGURE 5.67
Organization Logo
settings with Choose An
Image selected

Customize app store

You can customize the Teams app store with your organization's logo, logomark, and custom background or color. Learn more

Organization logo

Lets you upload a logo for your organization. The logo you choose will appear in the custom apps page in the Teams app store. Learn more

○ Don't show logo (default)

● Choose an image

Upload

This will be scaled to 240x60 pixels. It must be in an .svg, .png, .jpg format and be no larger that 5 MB.

FIGURE 5.68
Organization Logo
setting showing an
attached company

FIGURE 5.69
Preview of custom logo
for the Custom
Apps Page

CUSTOMIZE LOGOMARK (SMALL LOGO)

The organization logomark is the setting where you can upload your small corporate logo to display as an icon next to the Build For Tenant section title. When you select the Choose An Image option, you can upload the file of your choice (see Figure 5.70). The logomark should be 32×32 pixels, or at least a square format that will scale down to a 32×32 size. The file size must be 5 MB or smaller and the supported file types are `.svg`, `.png`, and `.jpg`.

FIGURE 5.70
Organization Logomark
settings with Choose An
Image selected

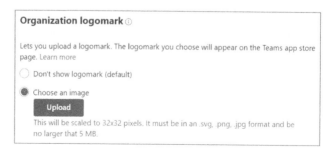

CUSTOMIZE BACKGROUND WITH IMAGE OR COLOR

Another setting you can customize for your app store is the background for the Apps ➤ Built For Your Tenant header. The options available for setting the background are to use the default Microsoft Teams app theme, an uploaded image, or a custom background color (see Figure 5.71). In this example, I chose a light sky blue, so now when I preview the results I can see the custom logo overlaying the background color (see Figure 5.72).

FIGURE 5.71
Background Image
setting showing
color selected

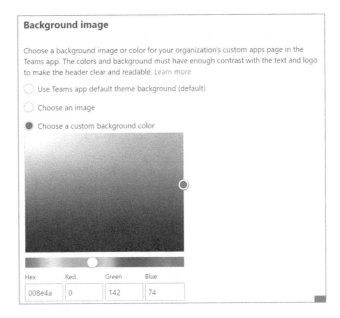

FIGURE 5.72
Preview displaying
custom logo and
background color

You can also use an image instead of using a custom color. The image must be 1212×100 pixels, and the restrictions are the same as the other image settings. The file size must be 5 MB or below, and the support file types are .svg, .png, and .jpg. Once you upload your background image (see Figure 5.73), you can preview the results to see how it will look (see Figure 5.74), and see the final result in the Teams apps store after the settings have been applied (see Figure 5.75).

FIGURE 5.73
Background Image display with JPG file that was uploaded

FIGURE 5.74
Preview displaying custom logo with custom background image

CUSTOMIZE TEXT COLOR OF YOUR COMPANY NAME

The last setting you can configure for your customized app store branding options is setting a custom text color that will display for your custom apps page. To set the color, you simply select Choose A Custom Text Color and then use the color picker or input the hex or RGB values (see Figure 5.76).

FIGURE 5.75
Custom apps store
branding displaying in
Microsoft Teams

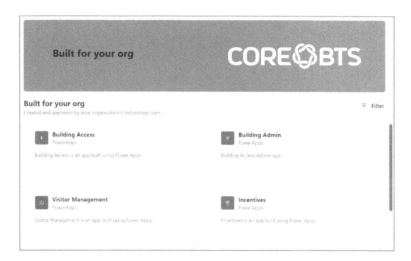

FIGURE 5.76
Organization name
custom text
color example

Analytics & Reports Menu

The last menu option we are going to cover in this chapter is the Analytics & Reports menu. This is where you can configure and see usage reports, reporting labels, and access the Call Quality Dashboard. The most used feature in this section is the usage reports. If you're a Microsoft Teams administrator, you can view usage reports based on the available drop-down options (see Figure 5.77). You can select 7, 30, or 90 days for the date range.

FIGURE 5.77
Usage Reports example

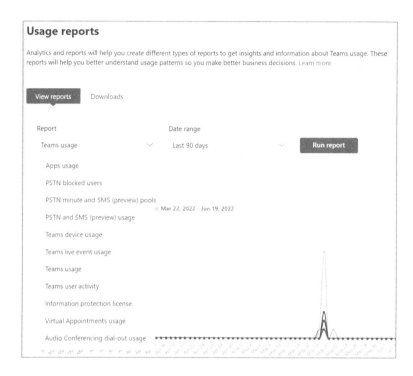

NOTE To learn more about reporting labels settings that are not covered in this chapter, please visit `https://docs.microsoft.com/en-US/microsoftteams/learn-more-about-site-upload?WT.mc_id=TeamsAdminCenterCSH`.

To learn more about the Call Quality Dashboard (CQD), which is also not covered in this chapter, please visit `https://docs.microsoft.com/en-us/MicrosoftTeams/cqd-what-is-call-quality-dashboard`.

The Bottom Line

Microsoft Team templates and template policies. Microsoft Teams come with pre-built templates to fit specific business scenarios. You can choose to use these templates as is or customize them to fit your needs. You can also create your own custom templates.

Master It You have users complaining that some of the pre-built templates they are seeing when creating a new team are not applicable to your business.

Content sharing policies for meetings. You are working with a consulting company that is a Microsoft partner who is helping you deploy a Microsoft 365 solution to your organization's tenant. You set up a meeting with engineering support from the consulting company using their email accounts. They join the meeting as external participants.

> **Master It** During the Microsoft Teams meeting you start sharing your screen to show the consultant the issue. You instruct the consultant to request control, but they inform you the option is disabled. Then you try to give them control and notice the setting is also disabled for you and is only available for you to select for participants who are in your organization.

Chapter 6

Security, Compliance, and Governance

The shift to remote work over the last two years has been one of the most significant changes in work culture. The modern workplace is more fluid today as many workers are no longer tied to physical locations. Organizations around the world rolled out Teams at a rapid pace as working from home became the new normal due to COVID-19. Teams has provided a way for organizations to adopt the remote/hybrid workplace to help their workforce collaborate more efficiently over long distances and in a fast-paced environment. As employees settle into a mode where they are either 100% remote or hybrid, most organizations are not prepared from a security, compliance, and governance standpoint.

The purpose of this chapter is to provide you with the general concepts for security, compliance, and governance for Teams. We will not cover how to implement global administration features, but we do include links to Microsoft documentation that provides steps for the global administrator to do so.

IN THIS CHAPTER, YOU WILL LEARN THE FOLLOWING

- ◆ Understanding the basics of Microsoft Teams security
- ◆ Compliance and governance for Microsoft Teams
- ◆ Privacy and Microsoft Teams

Security

Teams enforces security through team-wide and organizational-wide two-factor authentication, and single sign-on through Active Directory. Files in Teams are stored in SharePoint and are backed by SharePoint encryption. Notes stored in OneNote are backed by OneNote security, and the OneNote files are stored in the SharePoint site of the team.

Identity Models and Authentication

Teams supports all identity models that are available with Microsoft 365 and Office 365, which includes cloud-only and hybrid. With cloud-only, user accounts are created and managed in Microsoft 365 and stored in Azure Active Directory (Azure AD). User sign-in credentials are validated by Azure AD. With hybrid, user accounts are typically managed in an on-premises

Active Directory Domain Services (AD DS) forest. Depending on the configuration, credential validation can be done by Azure AD, AD DS, or with a federated identity provider. The hybrid model uses directory synchronization to sync user accounts from on-premises AD DS to Azure AD with Azure AD Connect. Most enterprise organizations have a hybrid implementation rather than a cloud-only implementation.

Multi-Factor Authentication

Technology makes it easy to sign into applications and cloud services with simply a username and password. The issue with password-only authentication is that passwords are the most vulnerable to cyberattacks, especially with online services. Unless you have complex passwords enforced within your organization, chances are many of your users choose a simple password and use it for most other online services as well. It is highly recommended to add an additional level of security for sign-ins with multi-factor authentication, otherwise known as MFA. MFA is supported with any Microsoft 365 or Office 365 plan, and the minimum recommendation is to require MFA for accounts that are assigned administrator roles.

It's highly recommended that you roll out MFA for all your users. Once enabled, when a user signs in for the first time after enrollment they will be prompted with a message that asks them to set up their additional verification method. Depending on your requirement configuration setup, your users can set up the following additional verification methods:

◆ **Text message:** A text message is sent to the user's mobile device with a one-time code, which they input into the login verification prompt.

◆ **Phone call:** Users can receive an automated phone call that verifies authentication when they answer.

◆ **Microsoft Authenticator app:** Users can install the Microsoft Authenticator app on their mobile device or tablet. They will scan a QR code for the initial setup and follow the prompts to finalize setup. The user can decide if they want to receive a prompt from the app to approve for sign-in or enter a code that is generated from the app.

Safe Links

Attackers have become more sophisticated in their attacks and in the ways they attempt to breach organizations and users. Many organizations have been educating their users on phishing scams, however attackers have been getting more sophisticated in their attempts to attack. Safe Links is a feature in Microsoft Defender for Office 365 that can be enabled to help protect your organization from malicious links that are used in phishing and other attacks. Safe Links is available for email messages, Office 365 apps, and for Microsoft Teams. M365 admins can create one or more Safe Links policies for your organization. Each policy can be configured to be scoped at the user, group, or domain level (see Figure 6.1).

Safe Links for Email Messages and Office 365 Apps

Safe Links protection for email scans incoming email prior to delivery for known malicious hyperlinks. Scanned URLs are rewritten using the Microsoft standard URL prefix: `https://nam01.safelinks.protection.outlook.com`. After the link is rewritten, it is analyzed for potentially malicious content. The URL remains rewritten even if the message is manually forwarded or replied to. This includes both internal and external recipients. Any new links added to a forwarded or replied-to-message do not get rewritten, but the original links remain rewritten. In the case of automatic forwarding by Inbox rules or SMTP forwarding, the URL will not be rewritten in the message intended for the final recipient. It will only be rewritten if the recipient is also protected by Safe Links, or the URL has already been rewritten in a previous communication.

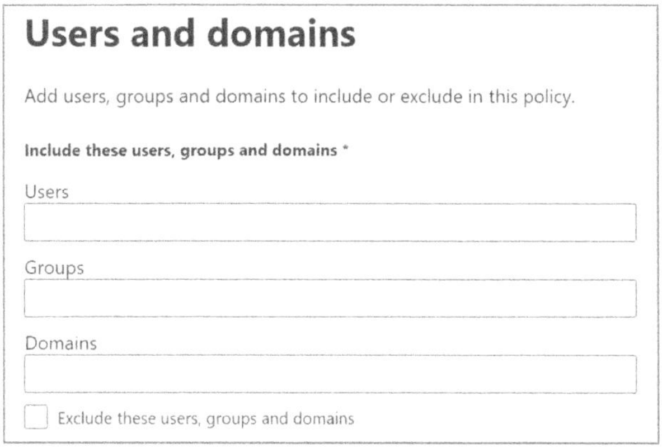

FIGURE 6.1
Users And Domains settings page for including or excluding in a policy

NOTE Safe Links capability requires Microsoft Defender for Office 365 licensing. To learn more, please visit `https://docs.microsoft.com/en-us/microsoft-365/security/office-365-security/safe-links?view=o365-worldwide`.

For more information on the Microsoft Defender for Office 365 service description, please visit `https://docs.microsoft.com/en-us/office365/servicedescriptions/office-365-advanced-threat-protection-service-description`.

For more information on the Office 365 plan options, please visit `https://docs.microsoft.com/en-us/office365/servicedescriptions/office-365-platform-service-description/office-365-plan-options`.

SAFE LINKS FOR MICROSOFT TEAMS

Once a Safe Links policy is configured and enabled for Microsoft Teams (see Figure 6.2), Safe Links help protect URLs shared in chats or conversations in channels. If a link is found to be malicious, users will have the following experience:

◆ If a suspected link is clicked in a Microsoft Teams chat or channel conversation, a warning message will appear in the browser (see Figure 6.3).

◆ If a link is clicked from a pinned tab in Microsoft Teams, the warning page will appear in the Teams interface within that tab.

Protection settings

Select the action for unknown potentially malicious URLs in messages.

○ Off

◉ On - URLs will be rewritten and checked against a list of known malicious links when
user clicks on the link.

Select the action for unknown or potentially malicious URLs within
Microsoft Teams.

○ Off

◉ On - Microsoft Teams will check against a list of known malicious links when user
clicks on a link; URLs will not be rewritten.

☑ Apply real-time URL scanning for suspicious links and links that point to files

☑ Wait for URL scanning to complete before delivering the message

☑ Apply Safe Links to email messages sent within the organization

☑ Do not track user clicks

☑ Do not let users click through to the original URL

☑ Display the organization branding on notification and warning pages

☐ Do not rewrite URLs, do checks via Safe Links API only. View supported clients.

Do not rewrite the following URLs

| http(s)://www.example.com | **Add** |

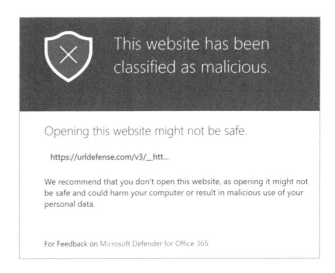

This website has been classified as malicious.

Opening this website might not be safe.

https://urldefense.com/v3/__htt...

We recommend that you don't open this website, as opening it might not
be safe and could harm your computer or result in malicious use of your
personal data.

For Feedback on Microsoft Defender for Office 365

NOTE For Microsoft's recommended Safe Links policies, please visit `https://docs.microsoft.com/en-us/microsoft-365/security/office-365-security/recommended-settings-for-eop-and-office365?view=o365-worldwide#safe-links-policy-settings`.

Compliance and Governance

Teams is built upon the Microsoft 365 architecture, which follows a regulatory framework that meets regional, industrial, and industry standards. Why is compliance and governance important? Organizations using cloud services store confidential data for their business need to configure additional security. Without good governance, your organization could be at risk of a data breach. Plus, home networks and BYOD devices open doors to data breaches and cyberattacks such as stealing a user's identity and gaining access into an organization. It is Microsoft's responsibility to protect the cloud service and it's an organization's obligation to detect and classify sensitive data. It is also the organization's responsibility to implement good governance and configure additional security and compliance policies.

How can this be done? Microsoft 365 offers a full suite of tools to maintain compliance as users collaborate in Microsoft Teams. Compliance controls include information retention, information classification, information protection, user segmentation, and data residency (see Figure 6.4):

- ◆ **Information retention:** Retain groups email and SharePoint content as well as chat and messages.

- ◆ **Information classification:** Classify groups and teams, automatically classify sensitive content, and encrypt sensitive content.

- ◆ **Information protection:** Prevent the loss of sensitive information, protect sensitive information in chat, and define your organization's sensitive information.

- ◆ **User segmentation:** Restrict communication between user segments.

- ◆ **Data residency:** Store data in specific geo-locations.

FIGURE 6.4
Microsoft Teams compliance high-level architecture diagram

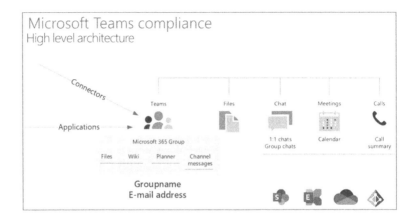

Compliance needs vary based on an organization's industry type. Organizations of all industry types around the world must follow different legal and regulatory business requirements. For example, U.S. banking and capital markets are subject to compliance requirements and guidelines from regulatory bodies such as the U.S. Securities and Exchange Commission (SEC), Commodity Futures Trading Commission (CFTC), Federal Financial Institutions Examination Council (FFIEC), and the Financial Industry Regulatory Authority (FINRA). U.S. financial institutions are also subject to laws such as the Sarbanes-Oxley Act of 2002 and Dodd-Frank. In North America, the energy industry is subject to reliability standards enforced by the North America Electric Reliability Corporation (NERC), referred to as NERC Critical Infrastructure Protection (CIP) standards. All bulk power system owners, operators, and users must register with NERC and must comply with CIP standards. Cloud service providers and third-party vendors such as Microsoft are not subject to NERC CIP standards. However, Microsoft customers operating bulk electronic systems are wholly responsible for ensuring their own compliance with CIP standards.

Regulatory standards recommended for consideration by energy organizations include the U.S. Federal Risk and Authorization Management Program (FedRAMP). Microsoft Office 365 and Office 365 U.S. Government tenants have been granted a FedRAMP ATO (Authorization to Operate) at the moderate impact level. Azure and Azure Government tenants have been granted a FedRAMP High P-ATO (Provisional Authorization to Operate), which is the highest level of FedRAMP authorization.

NOTE For more information about Microsoft cloud services and FedRAMP, please visit `https://docs.microsoft.com/en-us/compliance/regulatory/offering-FedRAMP`.

For more information about Microsoft Audit Reports please visit `https://servicetrust.microsoft.com/ViewPage/MSComplianceGuideV3?docTab=7027ead0-3d6b-11e9-b9e1-290b1eb4cdeb`.

Information Retention

Many organizations have requirements to retain content either for a set period or indefinitely. For example, let's say you have a business justification or regulatory requirement that all conversations and documents must be retained for five years. Your requirement during the retention period is that all information can be modified or deleted, but a copy of the information must be retained for five years. The requirement after the retention period is over is that the information must be deleted. To make this scenario work, you will need to use Microsoft 365 retention policies.

Retention policies and retention labels help you to manage information more effectively in your organization. You can configure retention settings to keep data that's needed to comply with industry regulations, legal requirements, or for your own internal policies. You can also configure your retention settings to delete data that is considered a liability, has no legal or business value, or is no longer required to keep. Microsoft Teams supports retention policies for chat and channel messages. The start of a retention period for chat and channel messages is based on when a message is created. You can apply a Teams retention policy to specific users and teams or to your entire organization. User-specific retention policies for Microsoft Teams do require the user to have an appropriate license such as an E3 or A3 licensing SKU.

Some organizations consider private chat messages to be more of a liability than channel messages, which are typically more focused on specific projects. Depending on your industry, regulatory laws or internal policies might require you to reduce the liability of private chats. What options do you have for configuring those policies? You can configure a single retention policy for all Microsoft Teams messages or configure for more fine-grained control by:

◆ Having a separate retention policy for private chats (1:1 or 1:many chats), messages from standard channels, or messages from private channels.

◆ Applying policies only to specific users or teams in your organization. For channel messages, you can select which teams to apply the policy to. For chat and private messages, you can select which users the policy applies to.

NOTE To learn about licensing for Teams requirements for security and compliance, please visit
`https://docs.microsoft.com/en-us/office365/servicedescriptions/`
`microsoft-365-service-descriptions/microsoft-365-tenantlevel-services-`
`licensing-guidance/microsoft-365-security-compliance-licensing-`
`guidance#information-governance.`

Information Barriers

Microsoft 365 compliance includes the ability to control the way people can or cannot communicate with each other. Information barriers are policies an administrator can configure to prevent individuals or groups from communicating. You may have a scenario in which you need to restrict communication and collaboration between different groups or departments to avoid conflicts of interest. Or you may have a need to restrict communication and collaboration between certain people inside your organization to safeguard internal information. You can do this all with information barriers. Microsoft Teams, SharePoint Online, and OneDrive for Business support information barriers. When information barrier policies are used, checks based on the policies configured are in place to prevent unauthorized communication and collaboration. Users who should not be able to communicate or share files with other specific users or groups will not be able to find, select, chat, or call the users they are restricted from communicating with.

For Microsoft Teams, information barriers can determine and prevent the following kinds of unauthorized collaborations:

◆ Searching for a user; preventing lookups and discovery of users in the people picker.

◆ Starting a 1:1 chat session with someone or starting a group chat.

◆ Adding a user to a team or channel.

◆ Inviting someone to join a meeting or placing a call.

◆ Sharing a file with another user and accessing files through a sharing link.

If users are included in an information barrier policy to prevent an activity, they will not be able to proceed. Some common industry scenarios for information barriers include educational, where a school wants to prevent students from being able to look up contact details for students from other schools. In professional services, an organization may want to allow chat with a client, vendor, or specific customer via guest access only during a customer engagement. Another scenario is in financial services, where investment bankers need to be restricted from communicating with financial advisors, but both segments are allowed to communicate with HR (see Figure 6.5). Your organization may want to implement barriers to prevent a team from communicating or sharing data with another team, or to prevent a team from communicating or sharing data with anyone outside of the team.

FIGURE 6.5
Information barrier
policy scenario

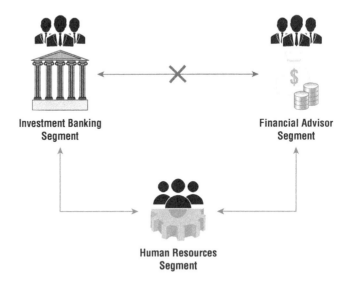

Retention Policies

In today's world, the volume and complexity of data in most organizations are increasing daily. This includes documents, emails, chats, and more. It is important to effectively manage or govern this information with the need to:

◆ Comply with internal policies and industry regulations that require you to retain content for a minimum period of time.

◆ Reduce risk in the event of a security breach or litigation.

◆ Help your organization by ensuring users are only working with content that is current and relevant to them.

Retention polices and labels help you manage the information in your organization more effectively. Retention settings can help you achieve these goals with two different actions: *retain content* and *delete content*. These allow you to configure retention settings for the following outcomes:

◆ **Retain-only:** Retain content for a period of time or keep it forever.

◆ **Delete-only:** Permanently delete content after a specified period of time.

◆ **Retain and delete:** Retain content for a specific period of time and then permanently delete the content.

Content in place is when the content remains in the original location when it has retention settings assigned to it. Most of the time, users continue to work with their documents and email as if nothing has changed when retention policies are in place. However, if they edit or delete content that is included in the retention policy, a copy of the content is automatically retained. For SharePoint and OneDrive for Business, a copy of the content is retained in a Preservation Hold library. Because Microsoft Teams is backed by SharePoint and OneDrive for Business for file storage, this applies to Microsoft Teams files as well. For Exchange mailboxes, a copy is retained in the Recoverable Items folder. For Microsoft Teams and Yammer messages, a copy is retained in a hidden folder named SubstrateHolds as a subfolder in the Exchange Recoverable Items folder.

NOTE The Preservation Hold library is included as part of the site's storage quota. The SharePoint tenant administrator may need to increase your storage when you use retention settings for Microsoft 365 groups and SharePoint.

Retention Policies for Microsoft Teams

Retention policies can be set up to retain and delete data from chats and channel messages in Microsoft Teams. As mentioned earlier, Exchange mailboxes are used to store the data being retained from chats and messages. The chat data in Microsoft Teams for each user is stored in a hidden folder in the mailbox of each user included in the chat. For channel messages, a similar hidden folder is used in a group mailbox. These hidden folders are designed to be inaccessible to administrators and users, but accessible to compliance administrators through search using eDiscovery tools.

NOTE To learn more about eDiscovery, please visit `https://docs.microsoft.com/en-us/microsoftteams/ediscovery-investigation?view=o365-worldwide`.

After a retention policy is configured for Microsoft Teams chat or channel messages, the paths the content take is dependent on whether the retention policy is to retain only, delete only, or retain and then delete (see Figure 6.6).

FIGURE 6.6
Retention period retain and delete diagram

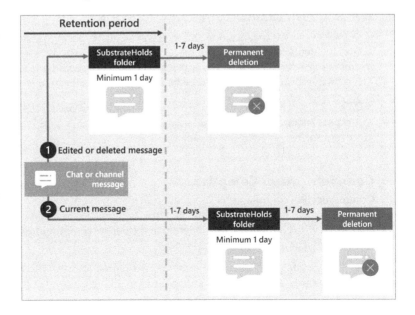

In this example, if a chat or channel message is edited or deleted by a user during the retention period, the original message is copied (if edited) or moved (if deleted). The message is stored in the SubstrateHolds folder for at least one day. When the retention period expires, the message is permanently deleted the next time the timer job runs, which is typically between one and seven days. If a chat or channel message is not deleted by a user and for current messages after editing, the message is moved to the SubstrateHolds folder after the retention period expires. This takes between one and seven days from the expiry date. The message is stored in the SubstrateHolds folder for at least one day, and then the message is permanently deleted the next time the timer job runs, which is also between one and seven days. When the retention policy is configured for read-only or delete-only, the content's paths are variations of retain and delete.

MEETINGS WITH EXTERNAL USERS

Channel meeting messages are stored the same way that channel messages are stored, so the location for the policy would need to be set to Teams channel messages. For impromptu and scheduled meetings, the messages are stored the same way that group chat messages are stored. So, the data location for this scenario would be Teams chats. When external users outside of your organization are added to a meeting that your organization hosts, the following occurs:

- If an external user joins by using a guest account in your tenant, messages from the meeting are stored in both the user's mailbox and a shadow mailbox that's granted to the guest account.

- If an external user joins by using an account from another Microsoft 365 organization, your retention polices cannot delete messages for this external user. The reason for this is because the messages for the external user are stored in the user's mailbox in their organizational tenant. Your retention policies will, however, apply to any of your internal users that have joined.

WHEN A USER LEAVES YOUR ORGANIZATION

If a user leaves your organization and their Microsoft 365 account is deleted, their messages that are subject to retention are stored in an inactive mailbox. The chat messages for this user are subject to retaining any retention policy that was placed on the user before their mailbox was made inactive. The content is also available to compliance administrators through an eDiscovery search.

NOTE   To learn more about how to set retention policies and labels, please visit
`https://docs.microsoft.com/en-us/microsoft-365/compliance/get-started-with-retention?view=o365-worldwide`.

Communication Compliance

Communication compliance is an insider risk management solution in Microsoft 365 that leverages machine learning to allow you to set up policies to help you overcome many modern challenges with compliance with internal and external communications. Here are some example scenarios for communication compliance:

- **Corporate policies:** In this scenario, users must comply with acceptable use, ethical standards, and other corporate policies in all business-related communications.

Communication compliance policies can detect policy matches and help you take corrective actions to mitigate these types of incidents. For example, your policy can scan messages in your organization for harassment, offensive language, or potential human resources concerns.

◆ **Regulatory compliance:** As mentioned earlier in the "Compliance and Governance" section, many organizations must meet some type of regulatory compliance standard as part of their normal operating procedures. For example, the Financial Industry Regulatory Authority (FINRA) requires organizations to have supervisory procedures in place to scan user communication and the types of businesses it can engage with.

◆ **Risk management:** Communication compliance policies can be used to help identify and manage potential legal exposure and risk. For example, your policy can scan messages in your organization for unauthorized communications and conflicts of interest about confidential projects.

Communication Compliance in Microsoft Teams

Communication compliance can be used in Microsoft Teams. If licensed, you can set up policies to help identify inappropriate content in public and private channels, 1:1 chat, and group chats. These types include:

◆ Adult, racy, and gory images

◆ Offensive, profane, and harassing language

◆ Sharing of sensitive information

NOTE For communication compliance subscription licensing/add-on requirements, please visit `https://docs.microsoft.com/en-us/microsoft-365/compliance/communication-compliance-configure?view=o365-worldwide#subscriptions-and-licensing`.

Before you can configure communication compliance policies you must enable permissions for communication compliance. To learn more on these requirements and steps, please visit `https://docs.microsoft.com/en-us/microsoft-365/compliance/communication-compliance-configure?view=o365-worldwide#step-1-required-enable-permissions-for-communication-compliance`.

Once you have your licensing and permissions in place, the next step for implementing communication compliance in Microsoft Teams begins with planning and creating predefined or custom policies to identify inappropriate activities. Microsoft Teams administrators can configure communication compliance policies at the following levels:

◆ **User level:** Policies at this level can be applied to an individual user or to all users within your organization. These policies cover messages that users send in 1:1 or group chats. Chat communications for assigned users are automatically monitored across all Microsoft Teams of which the users are members.

◆ **Teams level:** Policies at this level are applied to private and public channels of the team you apply it to. You can apply this to individual teams or to all teams within Microsoft Teams. These policies only cover messages sent in a channel and *do not* apply to 1:1 and group chats.

When you create a new policy you can start building it as a custom policy or choose from a predefined list. To block sensitive content, choose Monitor for Sensitive Info from the drop-down menu (see Figure 6.7). Then choose if you want to target select users or all users (see Figure 6.8). Next you'll need to choose the locations to monitor (see Figure 6.9) and the desired communication direction (see Figure 6.10) for the policy then continue to create. Once created, the policy can take up to 24 hours to go into effect. In this policy example, anytime a user sends a message containing sensitive content (such as an IP address) the DLP policy will display a blocked message similar to Figure 6.11. Recipients of the message will also see a message similar to Figure 6.12.

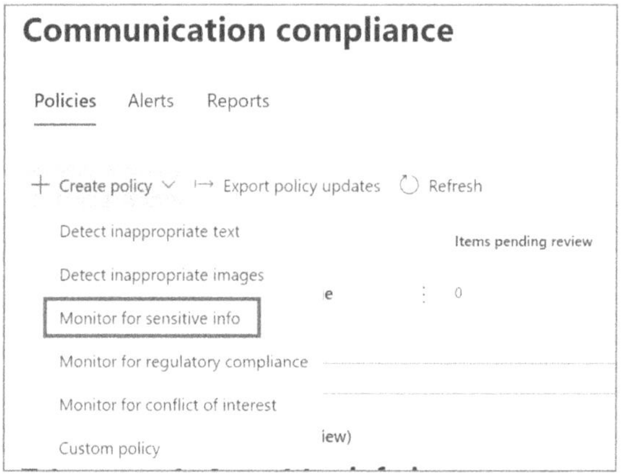

FIGURE 6.7
Create Policy sections of the Communication compliance page

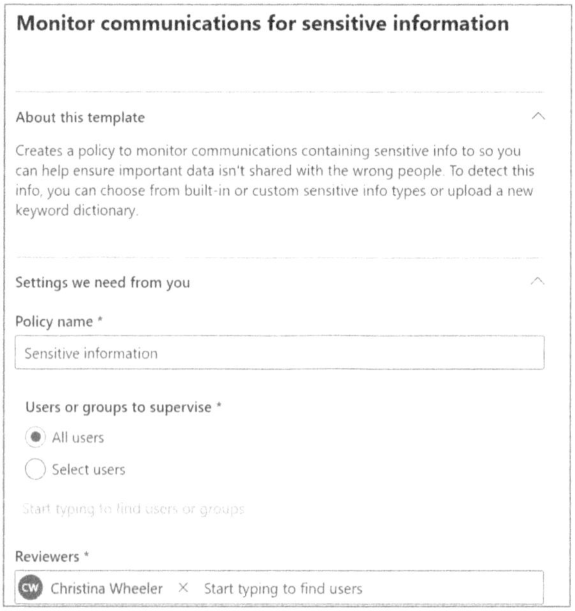

FIGURE 6.8
Setting a policy to monitor sensitive content

FIGURE 6.9
Choice of locations the
policy will monitor

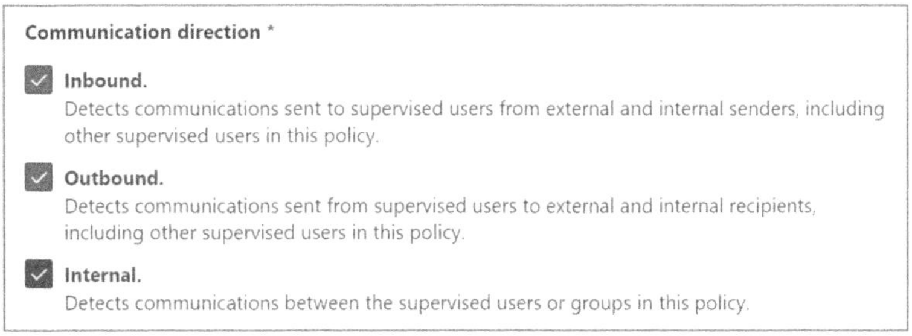

Choose locations to monitor communications

Microsoft 365 locations

- ✓ **Exchange.** ⓘ
  Emails and attachments sent or received by Exchange mailboxes.

- ✓ **Teams.**
  Messages in Teams channels and individual and group chats.

- ✓ **Yammer**
  Private messages and community conversations.

Non-Microsoft apps

Your org isn't currently importing communications from any non-Microsoft apps, such as Slack and WhatsApp. Learn how to create connectors.

FIGURE 6.10
Communication
direction options
for policy

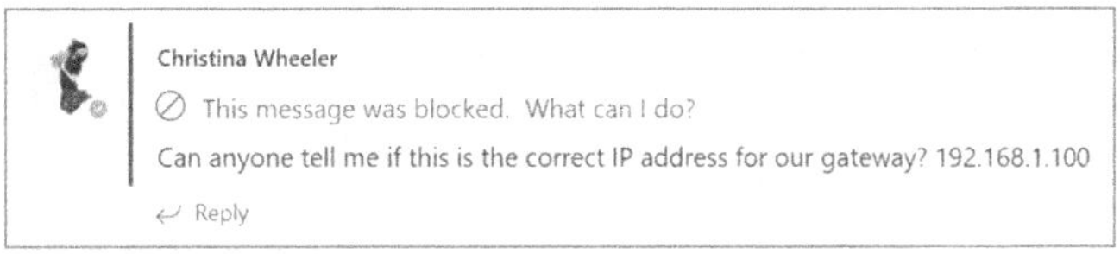

Communication direction *

- ✓ **Inbound.**
  Detects communications sent to supervised users from external and internal senders, including other supervised users in this policy.

- ✓ **Outbound.**
  Detects communications sent from supervised users to external and internal recipients, including other supervised users in this policy.

- ✓ **Internal.**
  Detects communications between the supervised users or groups in this policy.

FIGURE 6.11
Message sender sees
when viewing blocked
message posted
in Teams

Christina Wheeler
⊘ This message was blocked. What can I do?
Can anyone tell me if this is the correct IP address for our gateway? 192.168.1.100
↵ Reply

NOTE   For more information on how to configure communication policies, please visit https://
docs.microsoft.com/en-us/microsoft-365/compliance/communication-compliance-
policies?view=o365-worldwide

FIGURE 6.12
Message recipients sees
when viewing blocked
message posted
in Teams

Policy-Based Recording for Calls and Meetings

Microsoft Teams enables users to record a call or meeting with a click of a button. This is known as *convenience recording*. While this option is convenient, you may have an organizational need to control recordings or set retention policies. Policy-based recording enables organizations to use administrative polices to determine when calls and online meetings should be automatically recorded, and retention is required by corporate or regulatory policy. The four different categories of recording functionality are:

- **Convenience recording:** Ad-hoc recording of a call or meeting initiated by an end user.

- **Functional recording:** Automated recording integrated as part of an end-user productivity solution such as live events or meeting transcriptions.

- **Organizational recording:** Administrative recording of employee communications for risk management and compliance requirements.

- **Lawful intercept:** Silence surveillance authorized by Law Enforcement Agency.

Each of these categories involves different requirements for how the recordings are initiated, what is recorded and where recordings are stored, who is notified, who controls access, and how the retention is handled. For convenience recordings, the user is the initiator that records per-call or meeting. The storage owner is the user who stores the recording in their OneDrive for Business storage, and they are also the access owner to the recording. Retention policy for convenience recording is optional.

For compliance recording, the initiator is the system admin who targets automatic recordings per user. The storage owner, access owner, and a retention policy are required. When users are under a compliance policy, they will be aware that their digital interactions in Microsoft Teams are being recorded. They will not be able to stop the recording, nor will they be able to access the recording once the interaction is completed. The recording becomes a part of the organizational archive, which becomes available to compliance and legal personnel for eDiscovery, legal holds, and other corporate retention uses defined by your organization. Compliance recordings are implemented in Microsoft Teams as shown in Figure 6.13. Compliance recording can be enabled on Microsoft 365 A3/A5/E3/E5/Business Premium and Office 365 A3/A5/E3/E5 users.

NOTE To learn more about legal holds, please visit `https://docs.microsoft.com/en-us/ microsoftteams/legal-hold?view=o365-worldwide`.

FIGURE 6.13
Compliance recording solution architecture diagram

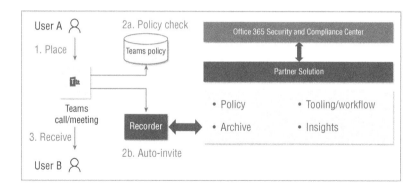

Sensitivity Labels

There is a way your organization can bring additional security and compliance to your collaboration environment through implementing data classification. Sensitivity labels allows administrators to set up policies associated with content labels that can be applied to your data to classify and protect documents, emails, and Power BI content. They can also be used to protect data at the container level, which includes Microsoft Teams sites, Microsoft 365 groups, and SharePoint sites. This added level of protection supports you with further security that includes:

◆ Deciding if Microsoft Teams sites, SharePoint sites, and Microsoft 365 groups can be private or public.

◆ Allowing or preventing external users.

◆ Allowing or preventing external sharing.

◆ Controlling access from unmanaged devices.

◆ Managing Default sharing link for a SharePoint site (this is a PowerShell-only supported feature).

NOTE Sensitivity labels are currently not supported in class teams for customers using Microsoft Teams Education SKUs. To learn more about licensing, please visit `https://docs.microsoft.com/en-us/office365/servicedescriptions/teams-service-description`.

Administrators can create, configure, and edit sensitivity labels in the Microsoft 365 Compliance Center (see Figure 6.14). Label options can be scoped at files, emails containers like SharePoint site, Teams and more. See Figure 6.15 for more options.

Edit sensitivity label

- ● Name & description
- ○ Scope
- ○ Files & emails
- ○ Groups & sites
- ○ Schematized data a...
- ○ Finish

Name and create a tooltip for your label

The protection settings you choose for this label will be
immediately enforced on the files, email messages, or content
containers to which it's applied. Labeled files will be protected
wherever they go, whether they're saved in the cloud or
downloaded to a computer.

Name * ⓘ

Confidential - FTE Only

Display name * ⓘ

Confidential - FTE Only

Description for users * ⓘ

Data classified for FTEs only. No external users allowed.

Description for admins ⓘ

Enter a description that's helpful for admins who will manage this label

Define the scope for this label

Labels can be applied directly to files, emails, containers like SharePoint sites and
Teams, schematized data assets, and more. Let us know where you want this label
to be used so you can configure the applicable protection settings. Learn more
about label scopes

☑ **Files & emails**

Configure encryption and content marking settings to protect labeled emails
and Office files. Also define auto-labeling conditions to automatically apply this
label to sensitive content in Office, files in Azure, and more.

☑ **Groups & sites**

Configure privacy, access control, and other settings to protect labeled Teams,
Microsoft 365 Groups, and SharePoint sites.

☑ **Schematized data assets (preview)**

Apply labels to files and schematized data assets in Azure Purview. Schematized
data assets include SQL, Azure SQL, Azure Synapse, Azure Cosmos, AWS RDS,
and more.

Choose protection settings for files and emails

Configure encryption and content marking settings to protect labeled emails and
Office files. Also define auto-labeling conditions to automatically apply this label
to sensitive content in Office, files in Azure, and more.

☐ **Encrypt files and emails**
Control who can access files and emails that have this label applied.

☐ **Mark the content of files**
Add custom headers, footers, and watermarks to files and emails that have this
label applied.

Auto-labeling for files and emails

When users edit Office files or compose, reply to, or forward emails from Outlook that contain
content matching the conditions you choose here, we'll automatically apply this label or
recommend that they apply it themselves. Learn more about auto-labeling for Microsoft 365

We'll also apply this label to files that match the same conditions in Azure Blob Storage, Azure
Files, Azure Data Lake Storage, and Amazon S3. Learn more about auto-labeling in Azure Purview

ⓘ To automatically apply this label to files that are already saved (in SharePoint and OneDrive) or emails that are already
processed by Exchange, you must create an auto-labeling policy. Learn more about auto-labeling policies

Auto-labeling for files and emails

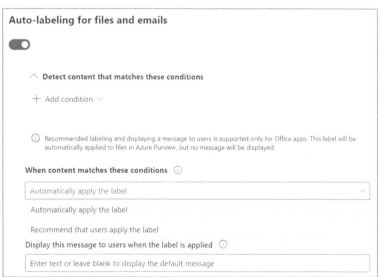

Auto-labeling for files and emails

⌃ **Detect content that matches these conditions**

+ Add condition ⌄

ⓘ Recommended labeling and displaying a message to users is supported only for Office apps. This label will be
automatically applied to files in Azure Purview, but no message will be displayed.

When content matches these conditions ⓘ

Automatically apply the label	⌄

Automatically apply the label

Recommend that users apply the label

Display this message to users when the label is applied ⓘ

Enter text or leave blank to display the default message

Once sensitivity labels are configured and applied with their associated policies, these labels
can be applied to teams within your organization. For example, when a new team is being
created the policy for a confidential sensitivity label can block a user from selecting public as a
privacy option. After the team is created, the screen will display data classification for the team
(see Figure 6.21).

Define protection settings for groups and sites

These settings apply to teams, groups, and sites that have this label applied. They don't apply
directly to the files stored in those containers. Learn more about these settings

☑ **Privacy and external user access settings**
  Control the level of access that internal and external users will have to labeled teams and Microsoft 365
  Groups.

☐ **External sharing and Conditional Access settings**
  Control external sharing and configure Conditional Access settings to protect labeled SharePoint sites.

Define privacy and external user access settings

Control the level of access that internal and external users will have to labeled teams and
Microsoft 365 Groups.

Privacy
These options apply to all Microsoft 365 Groups and teams that have this label applied.
When applied, these settings will replace any existing privacy settings for the team or group.
If the label is removed, users can change it again.

○ Public
  Anyone in your organization can access the group or team (including content) and add members.

◉ Private
  Only team owners and members can access the group or team, and only owners can add members.

○ None
  Team and group members can set the privacy settings themselves

External user access

☐ Let Microsoft 365 Group owners add people outside your organization to the group as guests. Learn
  about guest access

Information protection

Overview   Labels   Label policies   Auto-labeling

+ Create a label   ⊡ Publish label   ○ Refresh

Name		Order	Scope	Created by
Public	⋮	0 - lowest	File, Email, Site, UnifiedGroup	Christina Wheeler
General	⋮	1	File, Email, Site, UnifiedGroup	Christina Wheeler
Confidential - FTE Only	⋮	2	File, Email, Site, UnifiedGroup	Christina Wheeler
Confidential - FTE and NDA External	⋮	3	File, Email, Site, UnifiedGroup	Christina Wheeler
Confidential - FTE and non-NDA External	⋮	4 - highest	File, Email, Site, UnifiedGroup	Christina Wheeler

When sensitivity labels are in place, the experience when creating a team changes for the
users. Users will be presented with a Sensitivity drop-down menu with options based on what
has been configured in your tenant (see Figure 6.22). You can have a policy set up such as Public
and force the policy to only allow the user to create a public or org-wide (only available based on
permissions) team (see Figure 6.23). Selecting General enables creating a Private, Public, or

Org-wide team (see Figure 6.24). Choosing Confidential - FTE Only enforces the user to only be allowed to create a Private team (see Figure 6.25) and then once created the users in the Team will see a message in the team (see Figure 6.26).

FIGURE 6.22
New team creation showing available sensitivity labels

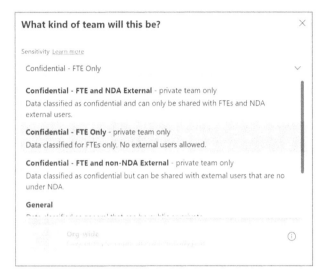

FIGURE 6.23
New team creation
Public sensitivity label

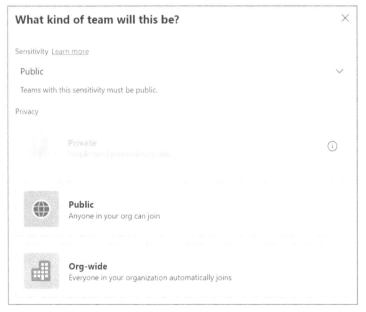

If configured and enabled in the tenant, users can be forced to set a sensitivity label when creating new SharePoint sites. When a user is going through the setup wizard, they will be required to choose a sensitivity label from a drop-down menu, as highlighted in Figure 6.27.

FIGURE 6.24
New team creation
General sensitivity label

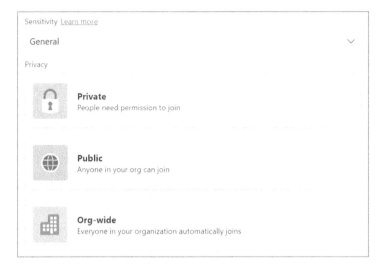

FIGURE 6.25
New team creation
General sensitivity label

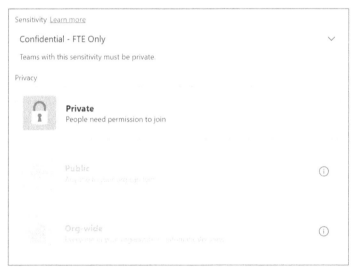

FIGURE 6.26
New team showing
Confidential sensitiv-
ity label

FIGURE 6.27
New SharePoint communication team site creation showing sensitivity label

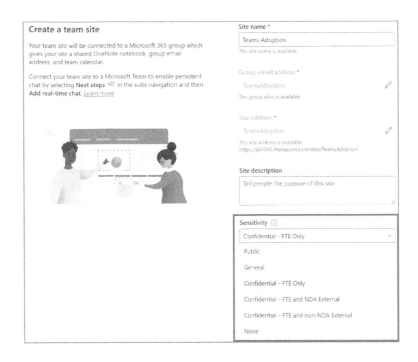

Create a team site

Your team site will be connected to a Microsoft 365 group which gives your site a shared OneNote notebook, group email address, and team calendar.

Connect your team site to a Microsoft Team to enable persistent chat by selecting **Next steps** ⬏ in the suite navigation and then **Add real-time chat**. Learn more

Site name *

Teams Adoption

The site name is available.

Group email address *

TeamsAdoption

The group alias is available.

Site address *

TeamsAdoption

The site address is available.
https://pbi365.sharepoint.com/sites/TeamsAdoption

Site description

Tell people the purpose of this site

Sensitivity ⓘ

Confidential - FTE Only ⌄

Public

General

Confidential - FTE Only

Confidential - FTE and NDA External

Confidential - FTE and non-NDA External

None

FIGURE 6.28
New Microsoft 365 group creation showing sensitivity label

Group email address *

M365Adoption   @pbi365.onmicrosoft.com

Sensitivity ⓘ

Confidential - FTE Only ⌄

None

Public ⌄

General

Confidential - FTE Only

Confidential - FTE and NDA External   s group

Confidential - FTE and non-NDA External   roup. Learn more about assigning roles to groups

☑ Create a team for this group

Back   **Next**   Cancel

NOTE While this book does not go into the global administrator role of deploying sensitivity labels, steps are required to support using sensitivity labels in your organization's tenant. Microsoft has detailed documentation online to support steps needed for deployment.

For enabling sensitivity labels for Office files in SharePoint and OneDrive for Business, please visit `https://docs.microsoft.com/en-us/microsoft-365/compliance/sensitivity-labels-sharepoint-onedrive-files?view=o365-worldwide#how-to-enable-sensitivity-labels-for-sharepoint-and-onedrive-opt-in`.

For details on how to deploy for Microsoft 365 groups to support container-level sensitivity levels, please visit `https://docs.microsoft.com/en-us/azure/active-directory/enterprise-users/groups-assign-sensitivity-labels`.

FIGURE 6.29
SharePoint site example showing label and policies applied

Data Loss Prevention

If your organization has data loss prevention (DLP) licensing, you can define policies that prevent users from sharing sensitive information in Microsoft Teams channels (public, private, and shared) and chat sessions. DLP capabilities for Microsoft Teams chat and channel messages, including private channel messages require the following SKUs:

- Office 365 E5/A5/G5
- Microsoft 365 E5/A5/G5
- Microsoft 365 E5/A5/G5 Information Protection and Governance
- Microsoft 365 E5/A5/G5/F5 Compliance and F5 Security & Compliance

DLP policies can be configured in the Microsoft 365 Compliance Center. You can start with a template or create a custom policy as well as filter DLP policy templates by country (see Figure 6.30). For example, you can setup a policy using the U.S. State Breach Notification Laws Enhanced template (see Figure 6.31) and choose the location to apply the policy to (see Figure 6.32). You can use the default defined settings (see Figure 6.33) or customize the advanced DLP rules. Additional settings include conditions for detection (see Figure 6.34) as well as what protective actions to take (see Figure 6.35) when a condition is met. New policies can be turned on right away, keep it off, or tested first (see Figure 6.36).

FIGURE 6.30
DLP policy category choices with country choices

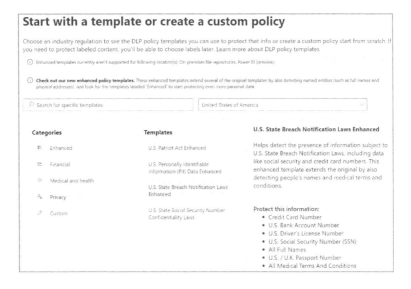

Start with a template or create a custom policy

Choose an industry regulation to see the DLP policy templates you can use to protect that info or create a custom policy start from scratch. If you need to protect labeled content, you'll be able to choose labels later. Learn more about DLP policy templates

ⓘ Enhanced templates currently aren't supported for following location(s): On premises file repositories, Power BI (preview)

ⓘ **Check out our new enhanced policy templates.** These enhanced templates extend several of the original templates by also detecting named entities (such as full names and physical addresses). Just look for the templates labeled 'Enhanced' to start protecting even more personal data.

🔍 Search for specific templates   United States of America ⌄

Categories	Templates	U.S. State Breach Notification Laws Enhanced
🏛 Enhanced	U.S. Patriot Act Enhanced	Helps detect the presence of information subject to U.S. State Breach Notification Laws, including data like social security and credit card numbers. This enhanced template extends the original by also detecting people's names and medical terms and conditions.
💶 Financial	U.S. Personally Identifiable Information (PII) Data Enhanced	
⚕ Medical and health	U.S. State Breach Notification Laws Enhanced	
🔒 Privacy	U.S. State Social Security Number Confidentiality Laws	**Protect this information:**
⚙ Custom		• Credit Card Number • U.S. Bank Account Number • U.S. Driver's License Number • U.S. Social Security Number (SSN) • All Full Names • U.S. / U.K. Passport Number • All Medical Terms And Conditions

FIGURE 6.31
DLP policy templates with U.S. State Breach Notification Laws Enhanced selected

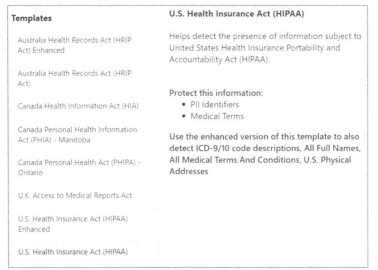

Templates

Australia Health Records Act (HRIP Act) Enhanced

Australia Health Records Act (HRIP Act)

Canada Health Information Act (HIA)

Canada Personal Health Information Act (PHIA) - Manitoba

Canada Personal Health Act (PHIPA) - Ontario

U.K. Access to Medical Reports Act

U.S. Health Insurance Act (HIPAA) Enhanced

U.S. Health Insurance Act (HIPAA)

U.S. Health Insurance Act (HIPAA)

Helps detect the presence of information subject to United States Health Insurance Portability and Accountability Act (HIPAA).

Protect this information:
• PII Identifiers
• Medical Terms

Use the enhanced version of this template to also detect ICD-9/10 code descriptions, All Full Names, All Medical Terms And Conditions, U.S. Physical Addresses

When a DLP is in place, policy tips will appear when an action is triggered from a DLP policy. For example, if a user attempts to share a Social Security number in a Microsoft Teams channel, they are prompted with a policy tip in Microsoft Teams (see Figure 6.37). When the user clicks What Can I Do?, a link opens a dialog box providing options for the sender to resolve the issue (see Figure 6.38).

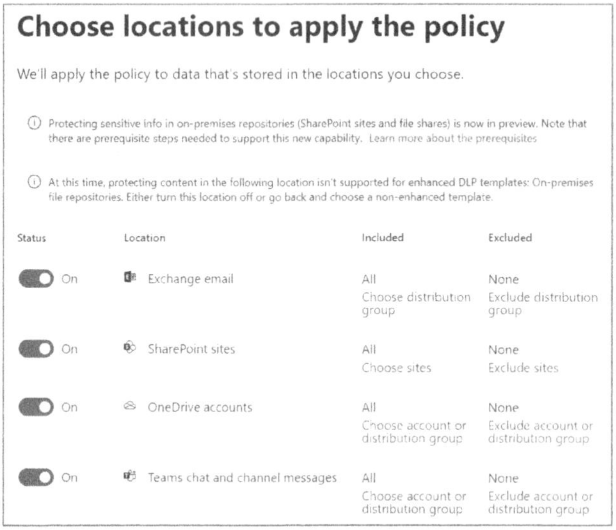

FIGURE 6.32
DLP locations to apply
policy showing all
enabled and disabled
locations

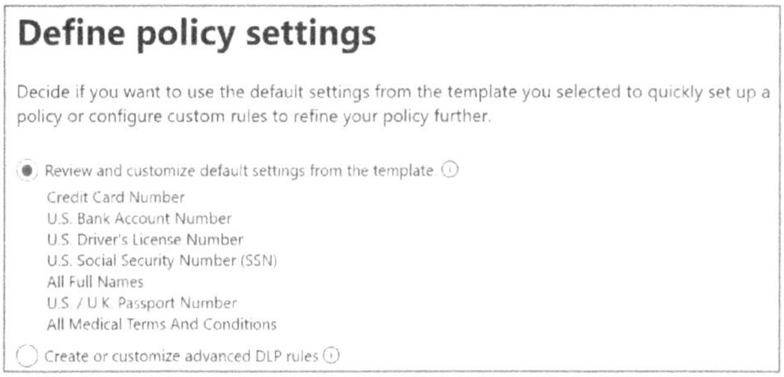

Choose locations to apply the policy

We'll apply the policy to data that's stored in the locations you choose.

ⓘ Protecting sensitive info in on-premises repositories (SharePoint sites and file shares) is now in preview. Note that there are prerequisite steps needed to support this new capability. Learn more about the prerequisites

ⓘ At this time, protecting content in the following location isn't supported for enhanced DLP templates: On-premises file repositories. Either turn this location off or go back and choose a non-enhanced template.

Status	Location	Included	Excluded
On	Exchange email	All Choose distribution group	None Exclude distribution group
On	SharePoint sites	All Choose sites	None Exclude sites
On	OneDrive accounts	All Choose account or distribution group	None Exclude account or distribution group
On	Teams chat and channel messages	All Choose account or distribution group	None Exclude account or distribution group

FIGURE 6.33
DLP Define Policy
Settings for
HIPAA example

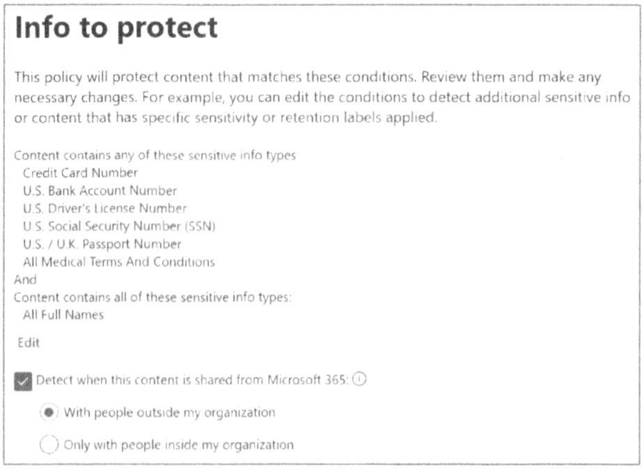

Define policy settings

Decide if you want to use the default settings from the template you selected to quickly set up a policy or configure custom rules to refine your policy further.

● Review and customize default settings from the template. ⓘ
   Credit Card Number
   U.S. Bank Account Number
   U.S. Driver's License Number
   U.S. Social Security Number (SSN)
   All Full Names
   U.S. / U.K. Passport Number
   All Medical Terms And Conditions
○ Create or customize advanced DLP rules ⓘ

FIGURE 6.34
DLP Info To Protect
settings for
HIPAA policy

Info to protect

This policy will protect content that matches these conditions. Review them and make any necessary changes. For example, you can edit the conditions to detect additional sensitive info or content that has specific sensitivity or retention labels applied.

Content contains any of these sensitive info types
   Credit Card Number
   U.S. Bank Account Number
   U.S. Driver's License Number
   U.S. Social Security Number (SSN)
   U.S. / U.K. Passport Number
   All Medical Terms And Conditions
And
Content contains all of these sensitive info types:
   All Full Names

Edit

☑ Detect when this content is shared from Microsoft 365: ⓘ
   ● With people outside my organization
   ○ Only with people inside my organization

FIGURE 6.35
DLP Protection Actions
settings for
HIPAA policy

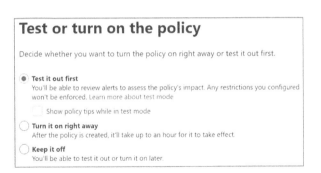

Protection actions

We'll automatically create detailed activity reports so you can review the content that matches this policy. What else do you want to do?

☑ **When content matches the policy conditions, show policy tips to users and send them an email notification**

Tips appear to users in their apps (like Outlook, OneDrive, and SharePoint) and help them learn how to use sensitive info responsibly. You can use the default tip or customize it to your liking. Learn more about notifications and tips

Customize the tip and email

☑ **Detect when a specific amount of sensitive info is being shared at one time**

At least [10] or more instances of the same sensitive info type

  ☑ **Send incident reports in email**

  By default, you and your global admin will automatically receive the email. Incident reports are supported only for activity in Exchange, SharePoint, OneDrive, and Teams.

  Choose what to include in the report and who receives it

  ☑ **Send alerts if any of the DLP rules match**

  By default, you and any global admins will automatically be alerted if a DLP rule is matched.

FIGURE 6.36
DLP Test Or Turn On
The Policy for
HIPAA policy

Test or turn on the policy

Decide whether you want to turn the policy on right away or test it out first.

◉ **Test it out first**
You'll be able to review alerts to assess the policy's impact. Any restrictions you configured won't be enforced. Learn more about test mode

  ☐ Show policy tips while in test mode

○ **Turn it on right away**
After the policy is created, it'll take up to an hour for it to take effect.

○ **Keep it off**
You'll be able to test it out or turn it on later.

FIGURE 6.37
DLP policy tip displaying
blocked message
to sender

MOD Administrator
⊘ This message was blocked. What can I do?
Typhoid meningitis SSN 199-50-7918 user3 DLP
↩ Reply

In this example, the user has the option to override and send a justification because the administrator who configured the policy set this as an available option. This setting can be disabled in the policy if your organization does not want to allow overrides. The recipient who was receiving the blocked information will see a message similar to Figure 6.39.

Your message was blocked because it contains sensitive data

- U.S. Social Security Number (SSN)
- International Classification of Diseases (ICD-10-CM)
- International Classification of Diseases (ICD-9-CM)

This item is protected by a policy in your organization.

Here's what you can do

Override the policy and send the message. or report this to your admin if you think the
message was blocked in error.

○ Override and send.

    Type your justification

○ Report this to my admin. It doesn't contain sensitive data.

                                                    Cancel   Continue

⊘ *This message was blocked due to sensitive content.* What's this?

↩ Reply

PREVENT SHARING SENSITIVE DATA WITH EXTERNAL USERS

DLP policies can also be configured to block sharing sensitive data with external users. To
support this scenario, your DLP policy needs to be configured with content conditions, sensitivity types you want to block, and detecting when content is shared with people outside your
organization (see Figure 6.40). The DLP policy will also need actions configured to restrict access
to the content for external users and notify users through email and with policy tips (see
Figure 6.41). When a user tries to share sensitive information that meets the conditions of the
DLP policy, the person sharing will be blocked with a message (see Figure 6.42). Let's say
someone copies or forwards a link to a guest via email or chat. If the guest attempts to access the
link, they will be blocked by the DLP policy and will see a message similar to Figure 6.43.

Choose the types of content to protect

This policy will protect content that matches these requirements. You can choose sensitive info types and existing labels.

| Default | | Any of these ∨ 🗑 |

Sensitive info types

Credit Card Number	High confidence ∨ ⓘ	Instance count [1] to [9] ⓘ	🗑
U.S. Bank Account Number	Medium confidence ∨ ⓘ	Instance count [1] to [9] ⓘ	🗑
U.S. Driver's License Number	Medium confidence ∨ ⓘ	Instance count [1] to [9] ⓘ	🗑
U.S. Social Security Number (SSN)	Medium confidence ∨ ⓘ	Instance count [1] to [9] ⓘ	🗑
U.S. / U.K. Passport Number	Medium confidence ∨ ⓘ	Instance count [1] to [9] ⓘ	🗑
All Medical Terms And Conditions	High confidence ∨ ⓘ	Instance count [1] to [9] ⓘ	🗑

Customize access and override settings

By default, users are blocked from sending email and Teams chats and channel
messages that contain the type of content you're protecting. But you can choose
who has access to shared SharePoint and OneDrive files. You can also decide if you
want to let people override the policy's restrictions.

☑ **Restrict access or encrypt the content in Microsoft 365 locations**

⦿ Block users from receiving email or accessing shared SharePoint, OneDrive, and Teams
files.
By default, users are blocked from sending Teams chats and channel
messages that contain the type of content you're protecting. But you can
choose who is blocked from receiving emails or accessing files shared from
SharePoint, OneDrive, and Teams.

   ◯   Block everyone. ⓘ

   ⦿   Block only people outside your organization. ⓘ

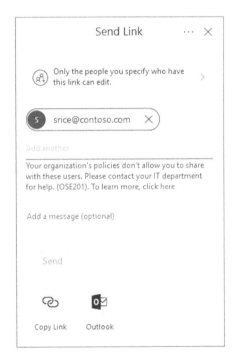

This link is only available to internal users

This link is not available to you.

TECHNICAL DETAILS

GO BACK TO SITE

Privacy and Microsoft Teams

When organizations are considering relying on or are already using Microsoft Teams for communication and collaboration, one topic that needs to be addressed at every level is privacy. *What personal data does Microsoft Teams collect? For what purposes does Microsoft Teams use this data?* The personal data Microsoft collects through Microsoft Teams is the following:

- **Profile data:** Data about you that is shared within your company such as profile picture, email address, and phone number.

- **Content:** Meetings and conversations, chats, voicemail, shared files, transcriptions, and recordings.

- **Call History:** Detailed history of phone calls you make, which allows you to go back and review your own call.

- **Call Quality data:** Details of meetings and call data are made available to your system administrators. This allows your administrators to diagnose problems related to poor call quality and service usage.

- **Support/feedback data:** Information related to troubleshooting support tickets or feedback submission sent to Microsoft.

- **Diagnostic and service data:** Diagnostic data related to service usage. This data allows Microsoft to deliver the service for troubleshooting, securing, and updating the product, and monitor performance. This also includes helping Microsoft with some internal business operations such as determining revenue, developing metrics, determining service usage, and conducting product and capacity planning.

For legitimate business operations, Microsoft will be an independent data controller for the personal data that that Microsoft Teams processes and will be responsible for complying with all applicable laws and controller obligations.

NOTE To read Microsoft's Online Services Terms, please visit `https://go.microsoft.com/fwlink/p/?linkid=2050263`.

Data Location in Microsoft Teams

Data in Microsoft Teams resides in the geographic region associated with your Microsoft 365 organization. For example, I'm located in the United States. You can verify (admin access required) where the data resides for your tenant by navigating to Microsoft 365 Admin Center ➤ Settings ➤ Org Settings ➤ Organization Profile ➤ Data Location. For my settings, Data At Rest is set to United States of America (see Figure 6.44).

FIGURE 6.44
Data location showing example of Organization Profile settings

Data location

As part of our transparency principles, we publish the location where Microsoft stores your customer content. For more information about Microsoft's contractual commitments, see the Online Services Privacy and Security Terms.

Learn more at the Office 365 Trust Center

Service	Data at Rest
Exchange	United States of America
SharePoint	United States of America
Skype for Business	United States of America
Microsoft Teams	United States of America

NOTE To learn more about where Microsoft 365 data is stored or to read about data locations stored for the European Union, please visit `https://docs.microsoft.com/en-US/microsoftteams/country-and-region-availability-for-audio-conferencing-and-calling-plans/country-and-region-availability-for-audio-conferencing-and-calling-plans`.

The Bottom Line

Securing Microsoft Teams with MFA.   Your company has implemented Teams throughout the organization to support the quick change to remote and hybrid working. You realize the rollout did not include enabling extra security for your users.

> **Master It**   With cyberattacks on the rise, you have concerns about your organization being compromised, especially with how fast your company rolled out Teams to all users. You want to implement additional security measures for all your employees logging in.

Retention policies for documents stored in Teams.   Your organization is gradually migrating documents from local file shares to Teams and SharePoint Online. As the rollout continues, you are working with each of the different departments to educate and help with the transition. During these transitions you learn that some of the departments have regulation requirements and concerns.

> **Master It**   The finance department received new regulation requirements and determined documents based on specific criteria that must be retained for a period of time.

Appendix A

Accessing Teams

This appendix shows you how to access Teams with a licensed or personal account through the browser, desktop app, and mobile app for both Apple iOS and Android devices.

Microsoft Teams App

You can easily access Teams with a licensed or personal account through the browser client, desktop, or mobile devices.

Browser Client

Accessing Teams through the browser is easy using your licensed or personal account. You simply open a browser and sign in to https://teams.microsoft.com. If you've already logged in to Office 365 through a browser, you can access Teams through the app menu. For example, if you sign in to www.office.com you can launch Teams by clicking the Teams icon on the left menu. You should see a Teams icon, and if you don't you can click the Apps button or click the app launcher (see Figure A.1).

FIGURE A.1
Teams options to launch in browser when signed into Office.com

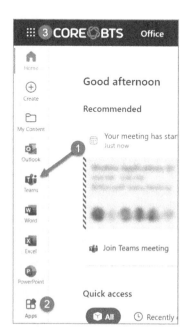

Once you click the Teams icon, Teams will load in the browser client (see Figure A.2). Here are some reasons to use the Teams browser client:

◆ You are prohibited from installing the Teams desktop client.

◆ You are signed in to the Teams desktop client with your organizational account but also need to access a tenant outside of your organization at the same time.

FIGURE A.2
Teams browser client in the latest Edge browser

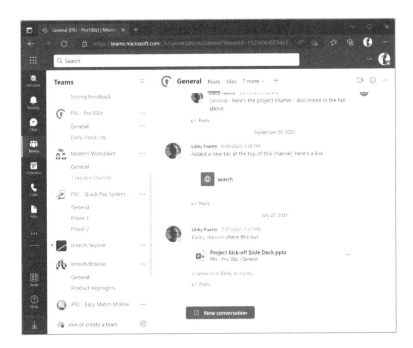

In some scenarios you might need access to multiple Teams environments. For example, you could be a consultant who has several Teams accounts for each client that you are actively engaged with on a project. You need to stay signed in to your organization's Teams environment and be logged in to your client's as well. In this case, you may want to use the Teams desktop client to log in to your customer tenant and use the Teams browser client for your organizational tenant, or vice versa. If you have been granted guest access to your client's tenants with your organizational account, you may want to use the browser to sign in to their tenant. Guest tenants would show up below your organization's tenant in the drop-down menu (see Figure A.3).

In this example, TeamsNation has granted you guest access to their tenant and has added all speakers and staff for their conference. Choose TeamsNation (Guest) from the drop-down menu, and the browser will then redirect you to their tenant and sign you in as a guest (see Figure A.4).

In this scenario, you need to be signed in daily to both your organization's tenant as well as the TeamsNation's tenant. You decide to use the Teams desktop client to stay in your organization's tenant (which in this example would be Core BTS) and then use the new Microsoft Edge browser for accessing TeamsNation (Guest). Since you need to do this daily, you can install the Teams browser client site as an app. At the time of writing, the following steps work in the Microsoft Edge browser version 99.0.1150.46 on both Mac and Windows. To install the site as an app, click the three dots (. . .), select Apps, and then click Install This Site As An App (see Figure A.5). You will be prompted with a dialog that allows you to edit the name of the app and then click Install (see Figure A.6).

FIGURE A.3
Organization tenant and guest tenants

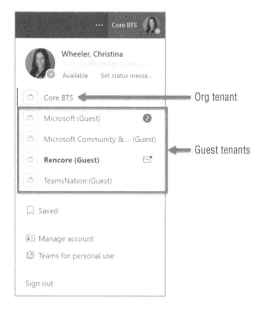

FIGURE A.4
Logging in to guest tenant in Teams browser client

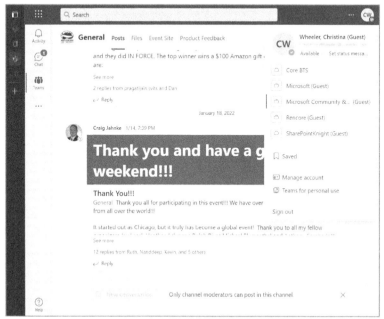

An App Installed dialog will appear where you can confirm or change settings. For example, you can pin the app to the Windows Start menu, add it as a desktop shortcut, and set it to auto-start on device login (see Figure A.7). When you're finished, click Allow, and you'll see your installed app in the Teams browser (see Figure A.8). You can access the app's info any time by clicking the three dots (. . .) located at the top of the app (see Figure A.9).

FIGURE A.5
Adding Teams as an app in the Edge browser

FIGURE A.6
Install app dialog example

FIGURE A.7
Setting the options for your app example

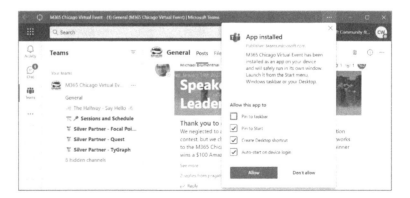

FIGURE A.8
App installed on the
Teams client browser

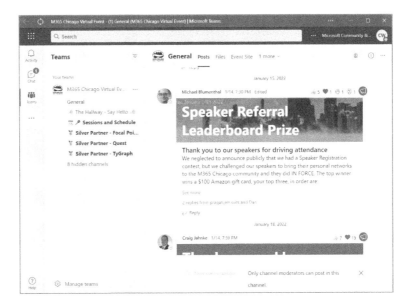

FIGURE A.9
Accessing your app info
in the Teams client
browser

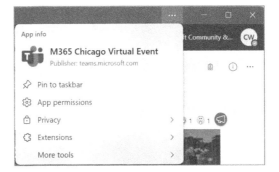

NOTE While you can use the browser client of Teams from a variety of browsers, some limitations exist depending on the browser. For more information on Teams client browser support and limitations, please visit `https://docs.microsoft.com/en-us/microsoftteams/get-clients?tabs=Windows#browser-client`.

Desktop Client

The Microsoft Teams desktop client is available for Windows, macOS, and Linux. To download directly from the browser, navigate to `https://teams.microsoft.com/downloads` from browser on a macOS (see Figure A.10) or Windows (see Figure A.11).

FIGURE A.10
Download Microsoft
Teams for macOS

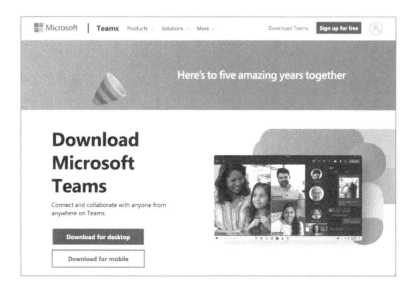

FIGURE A.11
Download Microsoft
Teams for Windows

If you are already signed in to Teams through the browser client, you can navigate to the drop-down menu and choose Download The Desktop App (see Figure A.12). If you are on a macOS, the file installer downloaded will be a `.pkg` file, and if you are on Windows it will download an `.exe` file (see Figure A.13).

FIGURE A.12
Downloading the desktop app

FIGURE A.13
Teams desktop client download for macOS and Windows

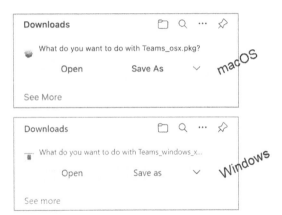

After the Teams desktop app is installed and launched, you will be prompted with a dialog to sign in (see Figure A.14). If you are signing in using your organizational account, click the Get Started button. To sign in with a personal account, click the Switch Teams App To Sign In Using A Microsoft Account link, located above the Get Started button.

To sign in with an organizational account, enter your password and click the Sign In button, or click Sign in With Another Account and follow the prompts (see Figure A.15). If multi-factor authentication (MFA) is enabled, you will be prompted to open your Microsoft Authenticator app to authenticate your identity (see Figure A.16). The Teams desktop client looks similar on macOS (see Figure A.17) and Windows (see Figure A.18).

FIGURE A.14
Teams desktop client log in page

FIGURE A.15
Signing in to Teams desktop client using an organizational account

FIGURE A.16
Multi-factor
authentication on the
desktop client

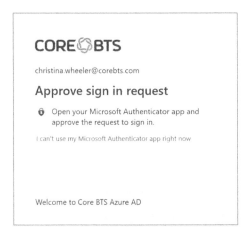

FIGURE A.17
Microsoft Teams
desktop app for macOS

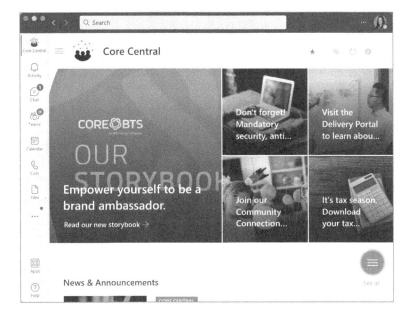

NOTE   For the list of supported operating systems for the Teams desktop client and for Linux
installation instructions, please visit `https://docs.microsoft.com/en-us/microsoftteams/`
`get-clients?tabs=Windows#desktop-clients`.

FIGURE A.18
Microsoft Teams
desktop app
for Windows

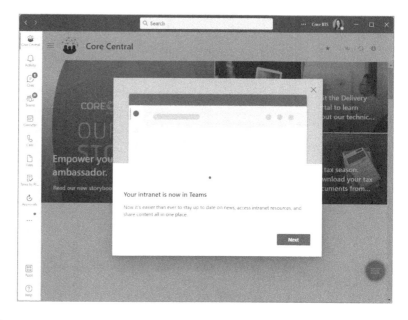

Mobile Client

You can install the Teams mobile app on both Android and iOS devices. Teams mobile apps are supported on the following mobile platforms:

◆ **Apple iOS**: Available through the Apple App Store on iPhone or iPad. Support is limited to the two most recent major iOS versions. When a new major iOS version is released, the new version of iOS and the previous version are officially supported.

◆ **Android**: Available through the Google Play store on mobile or tablet devices. Support is limited to the last four major versions of Android. When a new major Android version is released, the new version and the previous three versions are officially supported.

You can install the app from the Apple App Store on an iOS device or from Google Play on an Android mobile device (see Figure A.19). After you install the app, you'll be prompted to sign in and authenticate your identity (see Figure A.20). If your device is registered to your organization and subject to policies that protect company data, you could receive the message shown in Figure A.21.

Once you are signed in to the Teams mobile app, you can change any of the available settings for the app. To change settings on your Android device, click your profile photo and then click Settings (see Figure A.22). To change the settings on your iPhone or iPad, click the gear icon located in the upper-right side of the Teams app (see Figure A.23). Some of the settings you can change on iOS and Android devices include appearance for dark mode/light mode, notification settings for blocking, scheduling quiet time, sounds, and more (see Figure A.24).

FIGURE A.19
Installing the mobile
Teams app on iPhone
and Android

FIGURE A.20
Sign-in dialog for iPhone
and Android devices

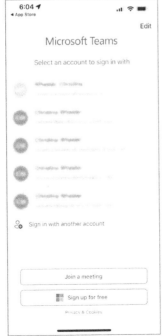

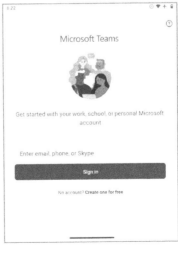

FIGURE A.21
Multi-factor authentica-
tion organizational
message for iPhone and
Android
mobile Teams app

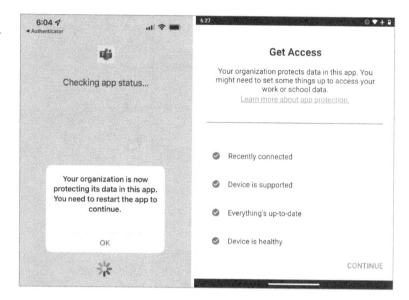

FIGURE A.22
Navigating to Settings in
the Teams app on an
Android device

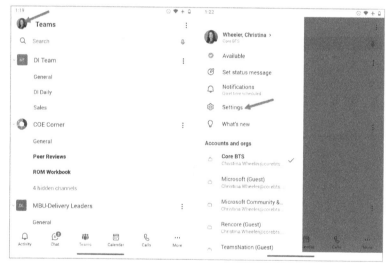

NOTE For more information on notifications and settings, please visit `https://support`
`.microsoft.com/en-us/office/first-things-to-know-about-notifications--`
`abb62c60-3d15-4968-b86a-42fea9c22cf4.`

FIGURE A.23
Navigating to Settings in
the Teams app
on an iPhone

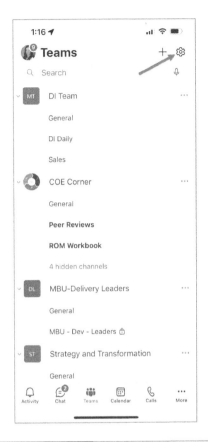

FIGURE A.24
iPhone and Android
mobile Teams app
Settings page

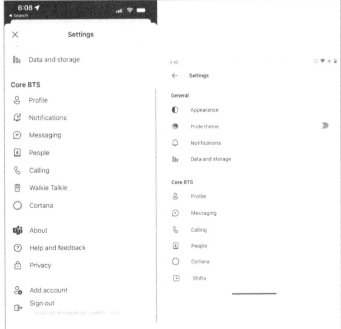

Appendix B

The Bottom Line

Each of The Bottom Line sections in the chapters suggest exercises to deepen skills and understanding. Sometimes there is only one possible solution, but often you are encouraged to use your skills and creativity to create something that builds on what you know and lets you explore one of many possible solutions.

Chapter 1: Getting to Know Microsoft Teams

Benefits of Teams   The modern workplace has changed drastically since 2020. Most employees, customers, vendors, and contractors are working remotely from their home where they miss the in-person collaboration or what we like to call "cooler talk." Microsoft Teams provides the flexibility of instant collaboration and empowers users to connect with colleagues and even people they need to communicate with outside of their organization.

Master It   Your organization has a vast majority of employees working from home or in other remote locations. There is a need to work with internal colleagues and outside vendors to complete their daily assigned tasks.

Solution   Use the Microsoft Teams client on desktop or mobile to provide a real-time and more personal experience to solve businesses problems by using chat, video conferencing, and file sharing to get the job done in a timely manner.

Environmental readiness and driving user adoption   The key to a successful deployment of Microsoft Teams is making sure the organization is in the highest readiness situation as possible. This includes ensuring that the planning, communication, and training being provided is seamless and transparent to the organization leadership, champions, help desk, and information workers.

Master It   The marketing department has a requirement to collaborate with a third-party video editing firm. They need to share marketing videos to be edited in a safe and secure manner.

Solution   The marketing department can use the Microsoft Teams file sharing capabilities powered by SharePoint. Since Teams is on the Microsoft 365 platform, the marketing department can add external users. This means they can share the videos with the third-party editors by adding them to a Microsoft Teams workspace as external users. By adding them, it will give the external users membership to the team just like a member of the organization.

Teams architecture   The Microsoft Teams platform was made for enhancing communication and collaboration in the modern workplace. Microsoft is constantly improving the platform to better enable organizations to streamline business processes, meet virtually combined with in-person meetings, and deliver an industry-leading solution for external sharing.

Master It   The production group has a need to train their employees to meet a regular compliance policy required by the federal government. They need to set up training sessions, provide employees with a registration form, and store the training recording in one place.

Solution   Microsoft Teams Webinars can provide the production group with a way to create training session based on a customizable registration form with all the great meeting features that a Teams meeting provides like chat, recordings, screenshares, PowerPoint live, and many more.

Chapter 2: Teams, Channels, Chats, and Apps

Teams and channels   The Teams workspace owners are empowered to manage their teams and channels in a manner that they envision. It is very important for them to manage the channels in a way that makes sense for the needs of the team members.

Master It   The training department has a request to organize, collaborate, and share existing files, and they have a need to create new files as part of their quarterly training assessments. They would like to use Microsoft Teams to manage their assessments, but they don't know how to organize channels. Currently, all their files are stored on a file share and they email updates back and forth with each other to collaborate.

Solution   The training department can provision a private Teams workspace to allow only the training department to access the files. Channels can be created for each specific topic to help organize their conversations and sharing of files. The ease of moving or dragging and dropping the files from a file share to Teams will help get the files in the correct channel file repository in the team. The training department can use the SharePoint library template feature to assist with new file creation based on a template.

Team membership and roles   The team membership and roles are defined by the Office 365 group created with the team. The team owner will need to decide who will be co-owner and who will be members of the team. The team owner will need to identify and assign users to contribute or assist with managing the team.

Master It   You need to allow members of your team to add additional members for a new project. This will assist you with making sure the right members on the team are added in a timely manner without you being the bottleneck.

Solution   As a team owner you can allow team members to request access for members of the organization to join a team. While a team member cannot directly add members to a private team, they can request someone to be added to a team of which they are already a member.

Managing teams   As an IT admin, one important task is understanding the life-cycle management of teams. As a team owner the life-cycle management goes beyond the administration controls and gets more involved with understanding the life cycle of content.

Master It   You are the team owner and have been asked to start planning the retirement of a team used for the latest completed project. You have been requested to retain the content and keep the team available for reference if needed. You will need to retain the team for 7 years.

Solution   As a team owner you have an option to retain the team and make the content read-only for the time required. You will need to archive the team. Archiving a team puts the team into read-only mode within Teams. Users will no longer be able to post conversation or files to the team and the content will be locked in View Only mode.

Working with channels   The channel feature provides a way for teams to be organized and structured by topics or common interests. The team owner can empower members of the team to manage specific channel components or sharing capabilities.

Master It   You have a few channels on your team for which you don't have the subject matter expertise at the channel level. You have several team members that do have the subject matter expertise at the channel level to best support channel moderation.

Solution   You can turn on moderation for a standard channel to give control to who can start new posts and reply to posts in that channel. Team owners can add content owners as moderators, which lets them control information sharing in that channel.

Teams templates   The teams template feature in Microsoft Teams provides flexibility for the IT admin and organization on whether they want to start with a predefined teams template or create one from scratch.

Master It   You have built a team structure with specific channels, tabs, and apps that provided value to a project team. You have been tasked with replicating that team for all projects for the future using Teams.

Solution   Microsoft provides prebuilt templates for reusable scenarios. You can create a team from an existing team, which will create a team that has the same channels, apps, and tabs. You can also work with the Teams administrator to create your very own template from your specific team.

Chapter 3: Meetings and Conferencing

Meetings in Teams   Teams makes it easy to collaborate with people inside and outside of your organization with the ability to meet with people using audio, video, and screen sharing. You can also easily add additional devices or transfer a device to a meeting you have joined.

Master It   You joined a meeting from your phone but during the meeting realized you need to present something from your computer. How can you transfer the meeting from your phone to your computer to share your screen in the meeting without having to hang up and rejoin?

Solution   When you are in a meeting on one device and decide to join from another, Teams will automatically detect you are joined and give you an option to add the additional device or transfer to the device.

Calls in Teams   You can start a call from a chat any time in Teams regardless if you are using the app or a browser. There are times when you may start a chat with a colleague and then decide to continue the conversation through a Teams call. This feature is great because it does not require you to schedule a meeting.

Master It   You are chatting with your colleague on an issue you are having, and your colleague decides to call you directly from the chat to discuss more. During this call you both decide you need to loop in another colleague to help provide feedback as well. How do you add another person to your active call?

Solution   You can add additional people to your Teams call at any time by searching for the person you want to call in the People panel. As soon as you add the person, Teams will start calling them so they can join your group chat call.

Live Events   Teams provides the ability to schedule live events. Live events are great to use when you need to have more than 250 attendees. When you create a live event it will default to the People And Groups permission level; however, you can change it to be Org-Wide or Public.

Master It   You need to create a public live event but the option to choose Public for the live event permission is grayed out. How do you enable your tenant to allow public live events so this option will become available?

Solution   All Teams tenants have default settings that can be changed through the Teams admin center. The default live events policy setting for who can join scheduled live events is set to Everyone in the organization. To enable allowing public attendees, you will need to change who can join scheduled live events to Everyone. Once it's set, it may take a few hours for the change to propagate. You will know it has propagated when the Pubic option becomes enabled.

Audio Conferencing   Teams provides an option where you can create meetings to include a dial-in number so attendees can call in when joining a meeting. This option is not available by default as it is dependent on an audio conferencing add-on license and configuration.

Master It   You have people both inside and outside of your organization that you meet on a regular basis. Some of the people are on the road and have issues joining through Teams. How do you make it easier for those who are on the road to call in without having to join from the Teams app or browser?

Solution   Purchase an audio conferencing add-on license for anyone who needs to provide a dial-in number for attendees during a Teams meetings. The license is only needed for those who do the scheduling and not org-wide.

Chapter 4: Extending Teams with Apps

Third-party Apps in Microsoft Teams   Microsoft apps, third-party apps, and custom apps in Teams makes it easier for you to combine your core workloads with your other systems and processes outside of Microsoft Teams.

> **Master It**   Your organization is using ServiceNow for your IT support outside of Microsoft Teams. Any time someone needs help they open a ServiceNow ticket from the website, which requires IT engagement. You discover there are common issues users are asking about that can be easily addressed without IT's engagement and want a way for everyone to self-diagnose and remediate issues. If an issue can't be resolved, then a ticket can be open.

> **Solution**   Install the ServiceNow app for Teams as an organization app so everyone can use it. Configure it to diagnose common incidents for self-remediation and only have it open a ticket if the issue hasn't been resolved.

App Templates for Microsoft Teams   App templates provide a great way to address business scenarios without having to develop an app for Teams from scratch. These low code/no-code prebuilt templates are available online for free and can be implemented into your organizational tenant.

> **Master It**   Users are complaining they are unable to create a team. Your organization disabled all users from being able to create a team and only the highest-level admins can create teams. You want to put a process in place to allow users to request to have a team created and have the request go through an approval process. Once approved, you want the teams to be auto-provisioned.

> **Solution**   Implement the Request A Team app template solution that was discussed in the "Request a Team Use Case" section of this chapter.

Chapter 5: Administering Teams

Microsoft Team templates and template policies   Microsoft Teams come with pre-built templates to fit specific business scenarios. You can choose to use these templates as is or customize them to fit your needs. You can also create your own custom templates.

> **Master It**   You have users complaining that some of the pre-built templates they are seeing when creating a new team are not applicable to your business.

> **Solution**   Navigate to the Microsoft Teams admin center and click Template Policies located under the Teams menu. Select any of the pre-built templates that don't apply to your business and then click Hide. Once you're done, click Save.

Content sharing policies for meetings   You are working with a consulting company that is a Microsoft partner who is helping you deploy a Microsoft 365 solution to your organization's tenant. You set up a meeting with engineering support from the consulting company using their email accounts. They join the meeting as external participants.

Master It   During the Microsoft Teams meeting you start sharing your screen to show the consultant the issue. You instruct the consultant to request control, but they inform you the option is disabled. Then you try to give them control and notice the setting is also disabled for you and is only available for you to select for participants who are in your organization.

Solution   In this scenario you will want to enable the Allow An External Participant To Give Or Request Control setting in the meeting policies for content sharing. Instead of changing this setting in the Global (Org-Wide Default) policy, it is recommended you create a new custom policy and then enable the setting mentioned here. Name your policy, save it, assign yourself and anyone within your organization who schedules meetings, and then enable this feature for their meetings.

Chapter 6: Security, Compliance, and Governance

Securing Microsoft Teams with MFA   Your company has implemented Teams throughout the organization to support the quick change to remote and hybrid working. You realize the rollout did not include enabling extra security for your users.

Master It   With cyberattacks on the rise, you have concerns about your organization being compromised, especially with how fast your company rolled out Teams to all users. You want to implement additional security measures for all your employees logging in.

Solution   In this scenario, it is highly recommended to enable MFA on your Microsoft 365 tenant for all your users. MFA is implemented at the tenant level and will require global tenant administrator permissions to implement. Once it is implemented your users will be prompted on their next sign in to provide additional information to set up MFA with the Microsoft Authenticator app.

Retention policies for documents stored in Teams   Your organization is gradually migrating documents from local file shares to Teams and SharePoint Online. As the rollout continues, you are working with each of the different departments to educate and help with the transition. During these transitions you learn that some of the departments have regulation requirements and concerns.

Master It   The finance department received new regulation requirements and determined documents based on specific criteria must be retained for a period of time.

Solution   Your first step would be to work with the finance department to gather all of the retention requirements. Then based on the requirements, you will need to set up retention policies in your organizational tenant using Microsoft Security and Compliance Center.

Index